*new
50 best
places to
enjoy
breakfast
and
brunch

By
Courtney Baron

universe publishing

Acknowledgments

Special thanks to Holly Rothman, my pancake-loving husband Blair Singer, and my many meal partners: Cheri, Brooke, Christine, Katie, Judythe, Lucy, Aashlesha, and Christian. I would also like to thank all of my fellow New Yorkers, who gave me great advice on where to go and what to eat. And, of course, my gratitude to Caitlin Leffel, an excellent editor with a great deal of patience, and Tricia Levi, my copy editor, for her superb work.

First published in the United States of America in 2005
by Universe Publishing
A division of Rizzoli International Publications, Inc.
300 Park Avenue South
New York, New York 10010
www.rizzoliusa.com

2005 2006 2007 2008 2009 / 10 9 8 7 6 5 4 3 2 1
Distributed to the U.S. trade by Random House, New York
Printed in the United States of America
ISBN: 0-7893-1355-3
Library of Congress Catalog Control Number: 2005015317

Publisher's Note

Neither Universe nor the author has any interest, financial or personal, in the establishments listed in this book. No fees were paid or services rendered in exchange for inclusion in these pages. While every effort was made to ensure accuracy at the time of publication, it is always best to call ahead and confirm that the information is up-to-date.

contents

introduction:
the most important meal of the day

By all accounts—doctors, trainers, nutritionists, and mothers agree—the morning meal is the most important meal of the day. In New York City, the options for this are endless. Every corner has a diner, every restaurant has its own spin, and every New Yorker can tell you a different place to get the best bagels. This book will help you navigate this vast culinary landscape. From corner coffee carts to four-star dining, and everything in between, *New York's 50 Best Places to Enjoy Breakfast and Brunch* gives you a taste of the interesting and exotic takes on the morning meal in the Big Apple.

In my research for this book, I discovered a couple of things about morning meals here that were different from the other places in the United States where I have lived, including Dallas, Austin, Seattle, Washington, and a small town in Arkansas. The major difference: the variety of options. In most of these other places, the morning meal is based on traditional American breakfasts: bacon and eggs, French toast, and omelettes. Even the fanciest restaurants and hotels in other cities tend to glorify the usual rather than explore new culinary territory. In New York, however, culinary adventures that we most often relegate to the dinner menu can be enjoyed for the morning meal at restaurants of all levels, all over town—from breakfast dives to brunch bastions and everything in between.

Another major discovery I made is that the benefit of morning meals in New York goes beyond nutrition alone. (Thank goodness!) A satisfying and enjoyable morning meal can set the tone for the entire day. After a romantic brunch at Dumonet, my husband and I walked hand in hand through Central Park. We hadn't planned our stroll in advance, it just naturally followed. One morning when I picked up a Jamba Juice on the fly, I realized that it left me extra time in the evening to make it to the gym. After breakfast at the Second Avenue Deli, I spent a happy while thinking of my grandmother, who was born on the Lower East Side. I realized that I had never been to the Tenement Museum, and that day I made plans to go. Take advantage of the neighborhood where you choose to have your meal, and let your restaurant choice guide your activities there. One of the great things about having a spectacular first meal is that it can easily lead into a spectacular day. I had many during the writing of this book; I hope it will lead you to your own.

the difference between breakfast and brunch

Breakfast is literally the meal that breaks your nighttime fast. For many New Yorkers on the go, however, it is the meal they pay the least attention to. Many skip this most important meal of the day altogether. But it's the fuel for your day and shouldn't be overlooked. The breakfast places chosen for this book can accommodate any lifestyle. Whether you grab a bagel with a schmear or have the time to sit down for bacon and eggs, take a fresh look at the first meal of your day. As often as possible, try setting your alarm half an hour earlier and ease into the day with a leisurely breakfast; you'll be surprised what a difference it can make.

Brunch, on the other hand, is a hybrid meal. It is a meal that begs you to sleep late and enjoy it as a replacement for both breakfast and lunch. Brunch is a weekend meal, most often relished on Sunday, although many of the restaurants listed serve brunch on Saturday as well. Unlike breakfast menus, many brunch menus are prix fixe and include libations such as Bloody Marys and mimosas; an alcoholic beverage is almost de rigueur. Because brunch is two meals in one, it is something one should linger over. It is also an excellent way to take advantage of some of New York's finer dining establishments, because brunch is likely to be cheaper than lunch or dinner. Another benefit: it's often more casual, so you can get away with wearing jeans to most of the places listed without worrying about how you stack up to the ultra-glam Friday night set. Brunch is also a great meal for a celebration, because there is something wonderfully decadent about enjoying a big meal—usually relegated to dinner—in the middle of a Saturday or Sunday afternoon. New York is one of the greatest brunch cities: not only is it one of the great gastronomic capitals of the world, but it's a city that understands that relaxing over a wonderful meal is the best antidote to a frenetic lifestyle. New Yorkers work hard, and should consider going out for brunch a reward for their efforts.

Around the World in a Morning

Most people think of dinner as the time to embark on a culinary odyssey, but in New York City, you can start your journey first thing in the morning.

Let's start in China with dim sum from the **Golden Unicorn** (page 87), then travel to Korea for a delicious breakfast soup at **Kum Gang San** (page 44), and then south for the Thai omelette at **Kittichai** (page 42). Moving on to another continent, there are all of the European morning-meal jewels, starting in the north with the Scandinavian herring and meatballs at **Aquavit** (page 72), moving south to Poland with the crispy, sweet blintzes from **Teresa's** (page 55), Austria with the pastries at **Café Sabarsky** (page 24), and west to France, which is represented at so many of the best breakfast and brunch places, from the Parisian café scene at **Pastis** (page 53) to the Provençal atmosphere at **Aix** (page 66). From there, you can jump over the Mediterranean to try the Moroccan eggs at **Café Mogador** (page 21). Then breeze on over to another part of the world altogether, to the Caribbean, where the spicy influence of Jamaica is in full force at **Maroons** (page 92), and then to **Calle Ocho** (page 78) where the flavors of Latin America are celebrated. Finally, make your way back to your native soil to sample the American classic comfort foods at **Amy Ruth's** (page 68) or **Bubby's** (page 18).

using this book

There are two sections—breakfast and brunch—each with twenty-five entries. Each entry has a tag line meant to give you an overall sense of the restaurant in a New York second, so if you're flipping through the book before you've had your first cup of coffee, you won't have to concentrate too hard to find a place to go: you just find one that fits your mood. Also noted are those entries that are particularly suitable for kids, celebrations, leisurely paper reading, or business meetings. Here are a few additional tips to help you make the most of your morning-meal experience:

❊ **Don't limit yourself to your neighborhood.** Most people I talked to don't venture far from home for the first meal of the day. I encourage you to hop on the train and make your morning an adventure.

❊ **Share.** Split orders of eggs and French toast with your companion—it's a no-guilt way to have both.

❊ **Try a solo breakfast.** Sure, it's the opposite of share. But I ate plenty of breakfasts alone and never minded a bit. In fact, I found it was a great way to get through the paper without interruption and to clear my head before embarking on the day.

❊ **Enjoy!** Don't let breakfast pass you by, no matter how busy you are. And use brunch as a way to unwind after a hard work week and to summon strength for the week ahead. You're a New Yorker, everyone knows how hectic your schedule can be, but taking the time to enjoy the first meal of the day, whether at 6 a.m. on a Monday or noon on a Sunday, can give you the energy you need to face the day.

breakfast

routine and exceptions

Breakfast in Manhattan can mean a thousand different things, from a bagel on the go to an elegant sit-down affair at the Ritz. The twenty-five choices in the Breakfast section reflect this variety. Most people have a set breakfast routine—whether it's scarfing a muffin on the train platform, cereal and Katie Couric, or going to a favorite eatery for "the usual"—and many of the choices here can easily fit into a New Yorker's breakfast ritual. Still, I encourage you to make exceptions to your rules. Woo a client with elegant bread baskets and your stellar business plan at a breakfast meeting at Michael's. If you know you've got a stressful day ahead, wake up early and engage in some preemptive decompression by stopping somewhere to read the paper over pancakes. You get three chances during the day to sample all of the culinary treats that New York has to offer, so don't miss out on some of the more interesting choices for breakfast. Breakfast is a great time to see the characters of this epic novel of a city at their groggiest. Everyone needs breakfast—just ask the USDA. So you might as well enjoy it!

1. Atelier

Putting on the Ritz never tasted so good.

✳ BREAKFAST HOURS:

Monday–Sunday 7–11 a.m.

Ritz-Carlton Central Park

50 Central Park South (at Sixth Avenue)

212-521-6125

Midtown

Good place for business meetings

Atelier, which opened in 2002, isn't just elegant—it's comfortable too. The perfectly appointed dining room with modern art flanking the walls reflects a deft attention to detail, but the atmosphere is entirely unfussy—a mean feat for a restaurant in the lobby of the Ritz-Carlton. The service is impeccable, so despite the grandeur of the room, you always feel like you're at a private table; this makes it an excellent choice for a business breakfast.

The menu is comprised of standard a la carte items and four "composed" breakfasts, which allow the diner to make a choice without having to work too hard. Their version of the perfunctory "Continental" stands out from the pack because of its superior selection of baked goods. The "American" consists of a baked goods selection with eggs, crispy-on-the-outside-creamy-on-the-inside thyme-roasted potatoes, and your choice of breakfast meats. The "Park" kicks it up a notch with eggs *en cocotte* (eggs baked in ramekins) with truffle jus, potatoes, breakfast meats, and baked goods. Be warned: the decadence of truffles at breakfast may inspire you to add the $25 caviar supplement. If you prefer your breakfast without the excess of the "Park" you may want to try the "Healthy Breakfast," which includes a bowl of beautiful fresh fruit and oatmeal or cream of wheat. All of the set breakfasts include freshly squeezed juice and coffee or tea. If the setting isn't tip-off enough, you'll know you're in capable hands when the coffee comes out, because the perfect brew is poured from sterling pots at the table (wouldn't want it to cool down even a fraction of a degree on its trip from the kitchen). If you asked for milk from a particular kind of cow, the kitchen probably would either have it on hand or have someone find it for you. This is the Ritz after all.

2. Balthazar

Jump-start your shopping day with a taste of Paris in SoHo.

❈ BREAKFAST HOURS:

Monday–Friday 7:30–11:30 a.m.

Saturday and Sunday 8–10 a.m.

80 Spring Street (between Broadway and Crosby Street)

212-965-1414

SoHo

www.balthazarny.com

Though New Yorkers aren't often inclined to agree (especially when it comes to food), few would dispute the following claim: Keith McNally knows breakfast. Three of his popular restaurants, Schiller's Liquor Bar, Balthazar, and Pastis, are included in this book. Balthazar, the eldest of the three, has endured flocks of tourists and hype, and now what helps this perfect replica of a *fin de siècle* brasserie maintain its charm is that it is a survivor, where the models that still come to graze are seated next to the rest of us mortals, and no one is given preferential treatment.

Well, that and the menu. The food at Balthazar never fails to satisfy. You could stick with the gorgeous pastries and sublime cappucino from the adjacent Balthazar Bakery and have a perfect meal without opening the menu. A morning that begins with a baguette spread generously with Nutella and a steaming bowl of café au lait is bound to be good. Or you could have the perfectly cooked soft-boiled egg served with toast "soldiers" to dip in the yolk. Whatever you have, breakfast at Balthazar is an enjoyable experience. Mornings are happily quieter than other mealtimes, so instead of waiting with fashionistas for a table, you can linger over your meal and indulge in people-watching at no extra charge.

Hey, if you squint slightly, the guy in the corner writing in his leather-bound journal may just be the next Rimbaud, shaking off a night of absinthe-drinking with a piece of quiche and strong coffee.

3. Barney Greengrass

A slice of smoked fish heaven.

❖ BREAKFAST HOURS:

Tuesday–Friday 8:30 a.m.–4 p.m.

Saturday and Sunday 8:30 a.m.–5 p.m.

Closed Monday

541 Amsterdam Avenue (between 86th and 87th streets)

212-724-4707

Upper West Side

Good for kids, if they eat smoked fish

Not long after he opened his restaurant in 1908, Barney Greengrass was declared "the sturgeon king." The restaurant, now run by grandson Gary Greengrass, has been considered a temple of smoked fish ever since. Name a fish and it's been smoked here. Offerings are paired with wonderfully pungent counterparts, like capers and raw red onions, and are served just about any way your kipper-loving heart could desire: on a chewy H&H bagel, scrambled with onions and eggs, or broiled and kippered with onions, among other options. For those insane people who don't love smoked fish, there is also a hearty selection of Jewish standards. Sweet cheese blintzes with sour cream or preserves (or both—in my opinion, the two condiments complement each other) could make any child happy.

And while the decor leads you to believe that the only things that have changed in almost one hundred years are the prices, you'll soon forget about the surroundings when the delectable smoked fish arrives. Barney Greengrass is classic New York at its best. Go to Barney Greengrass, and after partaking of the sturgeon on rye with raw onions or the whitefish salad washed down with a Dr. Brown's, and experiencing the brusque "Get-your-elbows-off the-table-food-coming-through!" service, no matter who you are, you come out a New Yorker.

Smoked/Cured Fish Primer

Smoking fish is an ancient method of preserving food. The remains of what is thought to be a fish-smoking "hut" discovered in Ireland are dated to 2000 B.C. And if you've ever had bad smoked fish, you might think it was smoked thousands of years ago in that Irish hut.

Smoking fish falls into two basic categories: cold smoking and hot smoking. As the names imply, cold-smoked fish is smoked at a relatively low temperature (85 degrees) for a long time. Hot-smoked fish is done at a temperature between 120 and 180 degrees for a shorter amount of time. Still, to smoke fish at home would take you at least a couple of days. Who has that kind of time? So go to Barney Greengrass, or hit the world-famous Russ & Daughters (179 East Houston Street between Allen and Orchard streets) to get some smoked fish to take home.

Here are some terms you might encounter when shopping for or ordering smoked fish:

kippered: fish that is split open, salted, and (usually) hot-smoked.

lox or gravlax: a Scandinavian-born variety of salmon that is not smoked at all; it is salt-cured. Lox and gravlax have a very delicate texture.

Nova: another word for cold-smoked salmon, named for its land of origin, Nova Scotia. Nova can be salmon of any type.

sable: smoked black cod.

sturgeon: a flaky white fish, usually smoked, and a source of caviar.

4. Bright Food Shop

Mexican and Asian done California (read: healthy) style.

❊ BREAKFAST HOURS:

Monday–Sunday 10–11 a.m.

216–218 Eighth Avenue (at 21st Street)

212-243-4433

Chelsea

Good for kids, vegetarians, and vegans

While it's not quite south of the border, there's a little spot in Chelsea that can warm your morning like the beaches of Puerto Vallarta, and present you with a plate of eggs that ought to be set against a Santa Fe sunrise. Bright Food Shop is a deceptively modest-looking little corner diner next to Kitchen Market, a great specialty grocery store owned by the same folks. The Mexican, southwestern, and Asian spices they sell there make their way into the eclectic fare served next door. Bright's breakfast selections include huge burritos filled with a choice of tofu; organic, locally grown veggies; or free-range chicken. The huevos rancheros are spicy, but not at all the typical lard-laden rendition of this dish found at most Tex-Mex haunts. The restaurant also has a great children's menu that should satisfy the most finicky *niño*, though if it doesn't, the staff is more than willing to keep the eggs from touching the beans. Bright Food Shop offers an exotic selection of juices ranging from organic pineapple to pure pomegranate, and it serves coffee made from organic, fair-trade beans. The restaurant has that special brand of early-nineties Mexican-inspired food with a healthy California bent, but there is nothing stale about this place. It's as fresh as can be, and it's a happy place to while away the morning . . . especially if you want to substitute tofu for the huevos without sacrificing any of the kick.

5. Bubby's

Celebrity sightings and comfort food are a fun combination.

❖ BREAKFAST HOURS:
Monday–Friday 8 a.m.–4 p.m.

120 Hudson Street (at North Moore Street)
212-219-0666
Tribeca

1 Main Street
718-222-0666
Dumbo

www.bubbys.com
Good for kids

I'm pretty sure that any place that starts as a pie company, as Bubby's did in 1990, will make the kind of breakfast I'm interested in consuming. Ron Silver's bastion to down-home cookin' (don't even think of adding the "g" here) is a favorite among Tribecans and tourists alike. (And, since 2003, for Brooklynites too.) At the Tribeca location, one hears a lot of talk of sightings of the neighborhood's prince-elect, Robert DeNiro, and his famous pals, but everything else at Bubby's is simply done and attitude-free. Celebrity hounds hoping to be starstruck still crowd in for brunch, but the breakfast menu is just as good, if not better.

The eponymous breakfast is the simplest and best choice on the menu: The "Bubby's" includes two eggs, home fries or grits, bacon, toast and "joe." The grits are creamy without losing their grainy texture, the bacon is thick and wonderfully smoky and salty, and if you are a home-fries person, you won't be disappointed by the restaurant's version—crispy on the outside, buttery on the inside. But let's not forget that it's the sweet stuff Bubby's started out with. Take out your insulin and enjoy a stack of the banana-walnut pancakes, best slathered with butter and luscious, real maple syrup. Health nuts will also feel welcome with the bowl of crunchy granola, served with yogurt, fresh fruit, and coffee (I guess granola isn't as chummy with joe). The sidewalk seating makes for perfect mid-morning people watching—if you can take your eyes off your plate.

In 2003, Bubby's opened a branch in Dumbo, which has become a popular breakfast spot as well.

6. Café Luxembourg

Enjoy bistro classics at a perennial Upper West Side favorite.

❊ BREAKFAST HOURS:

Monday–Friday 8 a.m.–noon

Saturday and Sunday 9–10:30 a.m.

200 West 70th Street (between West End and Amsterdam avenues)

212-873-7411

Upper West Side

Before Ouest, Aix, and Nice Matin, Café Luxembourg was the place to go for French food on the Upper West Side. It still is a low-key place to dine alone or with a group. The lemon yellow walls and classic Parisian bistro decor are warm on a chilly winter morning, or bright and sunny on a warm spring day. You can't go wrong with a simple breakfast of a pot of coffee and the scones du jour. The dense, buttery scones are given a Gallic flair with a dollop of clotted cream, which bears a strong resemblance to crème fraîche. If your sweet tooth is up early, try the warm sticky bun. Its ooey-gooeyness is kept in check by the hearty, yeasty bun. An elegant plate of grilled asparagus, just this side of crunchy, is served with fried eggs, lardons, and a hint of truffle. Café Luxembourg is a neighborhood restaurant. When I was there I saw a man come in, sit down, and have his meal served to him without a glance at the menu or conversation with the waiter. Whether you're a regular who lives around the corner or a first-timer from another borough, you'll want to have breakfast there every morning, not just because the food is so good, but because that kind of familiarity is even more comforting than a sticky bun.

7. Café Mogador

Take a morning trip to Morocco in this laid-back lair.

❄ BREAKFAST HOURS:

Monday–Sunday 9 a.m.–4 p.m.

101 St. Mark's Place (between Avenue A and First Avenue)

212-677-2226

East Village

Good for leisurely newspaper reading

First things first: order the Turkish coffee. Then close your eyes and wait for it to come to the table. (Your nose will alert you when it arrives.) Take a sip of the thick, grainy perfection, and you'll instantly feel revived, and a million miles away from the nearest Starbucks . . .

Now that you're awake, you're in the right frame of mind to choose your meal. You could have the French toast, which is great, but since you are at this cool East Village Moroccan dive, why not try something new? I recommend the eggs: *haloumi* eggs (poached eggs with delicious haloumi cheese, olives, salad, and pita), Middle Eastern eggs (two eggs, hummus, tabouli, and a spice blend of sesame, thyme, and *sumac* called *za'atar*) or, my favorite, the Moroccan eggs (poached eggs with Mogador's own spicy green pepper and tomato sauce). The portions are big and the service is exactly how you want it to be: unhurried and conducive to a leisurely meal. The cozy, cavelike rooms are tinged with a mix of bistro and something decidedly more foreign, transporting you to an exciting, unfamiliar world.

If you still want to linger a little longer after you're done eating (not that anyone at Café Mogador would ever think of hurrying you out), try a Moroccan tea. When the warm minty tea hits you, you'll want to open up the international news section, and make room for another plate of Moroccan eggs.

Bagel Wars

One of the greatest pleasures of a New York morning is a piping hot bagel with schmear. Sure, you can get a decent bagel in Milwaukee or Dallas, but here in New York you get something more—and I'm not just talking about the amount of dough. You get history. You also become enmeshed in a divisive debate: determining which shop makes the best, most authentic bagels. I've seen people get close to fisticuffs over this issue. Is it H&H? Ess-a-Bagel? And what about those Absolute Bagels that everyone is talking about?

Bagels have long had a special place in New York culinary history. According to some historians, bagels came to New York in the 1880s with the huge influx of Eastern European Jewish immigrants. Using recipes from the old country, bagel bakers hawked their goods on the streets of the Lower East Side. By 1907, the popularity of the bagel business created the need for the formation of the International Bagel Bakers Union. So, the bagel wars have been a long time in the making, and it's easy to be a willing soldier in the incursion, trust me.

H&H Bagels, founded in 1972, serves a particularly chewy version of the historic roll. H&H doesn't cut the bagels or toast them in the store. That's your job. They do sell spreads, but they are packed in small containers that you must deal with once you leave the store. But this doesn't bother the many fans of these bagels, who would say that a hot, fresh bagel may best be enjoyed in its natural state.

Ess-a-Bagel (which means "eat a bagel" in Yiddish) was founded in 1974, just two years after H&H. Ess-a-Bagel bakes its hand-rolled bagels according to old Austrian recipes, and its bagels are perfectly crisp on the outside with a dense (but not quite as chewy as H&H) inside. Ess-a-Bagel sells over two dozen different schmear concoctions, including tofu versions for the lactose intolerant or health-conscious.

A newcomer to the bagel wars is **Absolute Bagels** in Morningside Heights. It was started in 1990 by Samak Thongkrieng, a Thai immigrant who started his bagel training at Ess-a-Bagel. Absolute turns out the doughiest bagels of the three mentioned here; the crispy surface protects a surprisingly soft and airy inside. Always ask for what's hot, because the hotter the better. (This is true of all bagels, actually.) Also, Absolute offers minibagels, which are great for kids (and adults who don't think they can handle a whole one).

H&H Bagels
Monday–Sunday, 24 hours
2239 Broadway (at 80th Street)
212-595-8003
Upper West Side

639 46th Street (at Twelfth Avenue)
212-595-8000
Hell's Kitchen
www.handhbagel.com

Ess-a-Bagel
Monday–Saturday 6:30 a.m.–9 p.m.
Sunday 6:30 a.m.–5 p.m.
359 First Avenue (at 21st Street)
212-260-2252
Gramercy

831 Third Avenue (at 51st Street)

212-980-4315

Midtown

www.ess-a-bagel.com

Absolute Bagels

Monday–Sunday 6:30 a.m.–8 p.m.

2788 Broadway (between 107th and 108th streets)

212-932-2052

Upper West Side

8. Café Sabarsky

Delectable Viennese treats in the wonderful Neue Galerie.

❄ BREAKFAST HOURS:

Wednesday–Monday 9–11 a.m.; closed Tuesday

Neue Galerie

1048 Fifth Avenue (at 86th Street)

212-288-0665

Upper East Side

www.wallse.com

Good for "ladies who lunch" and art lovers

When my good friend Cheri said, "Go to Café Sabarsky," I said, "I'll try." When she took my arm and led me there, I said, "Really, that good?" She said, "You'll see."

She was right. Café Sabarsky is truly one of the most charming cafés I have ever been to. It is a gorgeous turn-of-the-century Viennese *kaffehaus* that is part of the Neue Galerie. The beautiful collection of twentieth-century German and Austrian art is housed in a stunning building on Fifth

Avenue, designed by the same architects who built the New York Public Library. The café is situated on a corner, so the picture windows offer a view of Central Park and serve as a happy reminder that you aren't stuck in the taxi-to-taxi traffic along Fifth Avenue. But while Café Sabarsky is on Museum Mile, don't expect the traditionally bland and artless fare of some of New York's other museum cafés. Café Sabarsky is presided over by chef Kurt Gutenbrunner, of the well-respected (and starred) restaurant Wallsé. The dining room complements the museum's collection with its Josef Hoff-mann sconces, Adolf Loos bentwood chairs, and Otto Wag-ner fabrics. The effect is transporting: you are suddenly in Vienna, and the rows of pastries on the bar near the entrance prove it.

Don't miss the soft-boiled eggs served in martini glasses. This is not a frilly touch; it simply makes sense to eat them this way (you'll see what I mean). The Sabarsky *frühstück* (break-fast) and Weiner *frühstück* both come with soft boiled eggs, as well as Viennese *mélange* (coffee), juice, and a crusty baguette (the "Sabarsky" adds thinly sliced Bavarian ham). For a sweet treat, try the *guglhupf* (marble cake), plain or hazelnut.

Be sure to plan enough time to view the Neue Galerie collection after your meal. (The museum opens at 11 a.m. on Saturday, Sunday, Monday, and Friday; it is closed on Tues-day, Wednesday, and Thursday.) The art is as delectable as the breakfast is artful.

9. City Bakery

A hip bakery/café that will satisfy your inner angel . . . or devil.

❊ BREAKFAST HOURS:

Serves breakfast-worthy items all day

Monday–Friday 7:30 a.m.–7:30 p.m., Saturday

7:30 a.m.–6:30 p.m., Sunday 9 a.m.–6 p.m.

3 West 18th Street (between Fifth and Sixth avenues)

212-366-1414

Chelsea

www.thecitybakery.com

Good for kids and leisurely newspaper reading

Soft, chewy pretzel, meet light, flaky croissant. Croissant, meet pretzel. Good. Pretzel croissant from City Bakery, meet your mouth. Even better. Now couple it with a small (unless you're sure you can handle more) hot chocolate, topped with one of the homemade marshmallows, and you've hit breakfast bliss.

If that all seems a bit elaborate for a morning meal, City Bakery offers some less decadent but equally satisfying choices. The oatmeal is thick and hearty, and can be topped with your choice of raisins, walnuts, toasted coconut, and other goodies from the oatmeal bar. There is also a selection of fruits, sometimes exotic, which is a nice accompaniment for bowls of plain or vanilla yogurt.

I've never been there when it was completely empty, but weekday breakfast is much more manageable than the weekend brunch crowd. I'd also say skip the counter breakfast; it's fine, but the pastries, oatmeal, and yogurt found at the back of the restaurant are fantastic. If you're alone, it's nice to sit upstairs and watch the bustle from the counter and stools that overlook the main floor. Behind the bakery counter there is an area for kids, with toys and books. The bakery is open and airy with an industrial feel, and there is no table service, so there is no need to feel guilty about lingering. On your way out, pick up a melted chocolate cookie. It's not a breakfast food, but it is sublime.

10. Clinton Street Baking Company & Restaurant

A cozy bakery/café for a late-morning meal.

❊ BREAKFAST HOURS:

Monday–Friday 11:30 a.m.–4 p.m.

4 Clinton Street (between Houston and Stanton streets)

646-602-6263

Lower East Side

www.clintonstreetbaking.com

One cold morning, my husband and I tucked ourselves into a tiny table at Clinton Street Baking Company & Restaurant. The sparsely decorated restaurant was suspiciously empty, but as we soon learned, we were simply early by neighborhood standards. As we took the first bites of our meal, some groggy, bleary-eyed hipsters began to slink in, with desperate looks that read "Coffee. Now." By the time we paid our bill the place was full. What's the rush? Most of the great stores in the area don't open until noon anyway.

There's a lot to love on Neil Kleinberg's down-home menu, but you'd be sinning if you missed the buttermilk biscuit sandwich with fluffy scrambled eggs, cheddar cheese, and homemade tomato jam on a flaky, buttery biscuit. (Add the bacon!) Or you could try the Spanish version with melted jack cheese, tomatillo sauce, and spicy chorizo. The restaurant can also please a pancake connoisseur with the wonderful Maine blueberry pancakes, so packed with plump fruit that they're bursting at the seams. You don't even need syrup—the warm maple butter they serve is the perfect topper. The bottomless cup of coffee is a great perk, as is the friendly, attitude-free service. On your way out, take a few of the superb scones to go to tide you over until your 4 p.m. lunch. Hey, this is the Lower East Side.

11. Delis

Carnegie Deli

Katz's Delicatessen

Second Avenue Deli

Because everyone has a favorite, and because all three are great . . .

Carnegie Deli

❉ BREAKFAST HOURS:

Monday–Sunday 6:30–11 a.m.

854 Seventh Avenue (at 55th Street)

212-757-2245

Midtown

www.carnegiedeli.com

Good for kids and kvetchers

Cash only

Katz's Delicatessen

❉ BREAKFAST HOURS:

Monday-Sunday 8–11:30 a.m.

205 East Houston Street (at Ludlow Street)

212-254-2246

Lower East Side

www.katzdeli.com

Good for kids and your cardiologist's summer home

Second Avenue Deli

❉ BREAKFAST HOURS:

Sunday–Thursday 7 a.m.–Midnight, Friday–Saturday

7 a.m.–3 a.m.

156 Second Avenue (at 10th Street)

212-677-0606

East Village

www.2ndavedeli.com

Good for kids and heartburn "like Bubbe used to make"

There are many similarities between these classic New York delis, but don't tell them that. Working our way downtown:

Carnegie is in the heart of Midtown, as it has been for over sixty-five years. Internationally renowned for its enormous sandwiches, breakfast portions there do not disappoint either. The Nova platter comes with enough smoked salmon to make you wonder if they'll single-handedly put the fish on the endangered species list. The salami and eggs (which my dad likes to top with melted Swiss cheese—don't let his doctor know!) is rich, greasy, and so yummy. If you want to sample the pastrami, try the huge pastrami omelette. The cook either uses more than the three eggs the menu promises or else he knows a mighty big hen. The atmosphere is shabby, the walls are covered in photos of the famous (and not-so-famous) celebrities that have eaten there, and the service is old New York all the way, replete with insistent "Hurry it up"s and reminders that "We charge for sharing." But hey, that's what makes it fun.

From there, hop on the subway and head down to the East Village to hit the Second Avenue Deli. The deli was recently given a face-lift, but don't worry, there's nothing shiny here but the schmaltz. The cheese blintzes are almost as good as they were at the much-missed Ratner's, and the potato pancakes are heavenly. I didn't have the tongue and eggs served "pancake style," but I'm glad it's on the menu. The *matzoh brie* (eggs scrambled with matzoh), is great, and especially tasty topped with a little applesauce. The Second Avenue Deli is a New York institution because whatever you crave, you can find it there, and it will be good.

You can walk to Katz's from the Second Avenue Deli (exercise is not a bad idea in between potato pancakes and pastrami). When you enter, grab a number (don't lose it or you'll be fined), and either line up or push your way to the back for table service. But once you get past the pomp and procedure and taste the pastrami omelette, you'll understand what made Meg Ryan orgasmic in *When Harry Met Sally*. The beef sausage has clearly come down from red meat heaven. The eggs with lox and onions comes with steak fries, a combination that is as good as it gets. Everyone looks a little confused about the system when they first come in, but once you get the hang of it, you'll feel right at home. That's the great thing about Katz's.

My recommendation: don't eat at all three in one day. As my grandmother would say, "Too much of a good thing can be bad, but too much of a great thing might kill you."

12. The Doughnut Plant

Yes, a doughnut can be a meal; in fact, here it can be a gourmet meal—trust me.

❄ BREAKFAST HOURS:

> Opens at 7 a.m., doughnuts usually sold out by 5 p.m.
> 379 Grand Street (at Norfolk Street)
> 212-505-3700
> Lower East Side
> Good for little kids and adult kids

I have this recurring dream: It's past midnight, and I'm standing on a pile of broken glass just inside a storefront on the Lower East Side. The high beams of a cop car are bright in my eyes, and a voice over a megaphone says, "Step away from the doughnut, ma'am. Step away from the doughnut."

When Mark Israel stumbled upon his grandfather's recipe for doughnuts about ten years ago, we all got lucky. If you thought there was no such thing as an artisanal doughnut, well, you're in for an unexpected treat. These criminally decadent doughnuts—sold at his shop on the Lower East Side and all over town at coffee shops and gourmet markets like Dean & Deluca and Whole Foods—are handmade in small batches. Their light and chewy texture puts mass-produced doughnuts to shame, and they are hand-glazed with the best and freshest ingredients. Like any culinary craftsman, Israel is inspired by seasonal offerings, which means pumpkin-glazed doughnuts in the fall and strawberry-glazed doughnuts in the summer (the glaze has chunks of fresh strawberries in it). The chocolate doughnuts are glazed with Vahlrona chocolate, and the vanilla are made with Tahitian vanilla beans. No wonder *Saveur* voted The Doughnut Plant one of the six best places to get doughnuts in the country.

While you can get the doughnuts at various retailers

around town, I recommend making the trek down to his shop on Grand Street. You could content yourself with Israel's treats alone, or indulge in a multiethnic gastronomic adventure. Start with the perfect doughnut, move on to Kossar's Bialys next door, hit The Pickle Guys around the corner (on Essex at Grand Street), and end with gelato from Il Laboratorio del Gelato (Orchard at Delancey Street) a few blocks away. What a day that would be!

13. Florent

Beat your hangover at this haute diner.

❉ BREAKFAST HOURS:
All day, every day.
69 Gansevoort Street (between Greenwich and
Washington streets)
212-989-5779
Meatpacking District
www.restaurantflorent.com
Good for late risers and up-all-nighters

It's 2:30 a.m. and you're starving. Sure there are plenty of choices for all-night dining, but few are as charming as Florent. Well, you're in luck, because this is the time when the restaurant starts serving the "Breakfast Special": two eggs, potatoes, toast, juice, and coffee for $7.50—the perfect antidote to a night spent drinking ten-dollar martinis. Florent Morellet's 24-hour joint has been feeding the masses—or, er, the artists, the socialites, the drunken whomevers, and the lonely guy with his copy of Kafka's *The Trial* in the corner over there—since before the Meatpacking District was a neighborhood. The decor is an eclectic take on classic diner design, and the staff is as welcoming as the sweet glowing neon sign in the window—a clear asset at 2:30 a.m.

But this is a diner that hasn't lost its sense of humor. The reason you go to Florent over your neighborhood joint is that your local diner doesn't offer the kind of creativity with breakfast fare that is found here. At Florent, the goat cheese omelette comes with apples, onions, and herbs, which balance the rich creaminess of the goat cheese. The French toast is dreamy, not too eggy and just sweet enough. You could also try the grilled cheese with bacon—even though it doesn't reside in the typical breakfast canon Florent's cheeky, carefree atmosphere encourages you to rethink the meaning of breakfast. Check out what's written on the chalkboard; you may be inclined to rethink a lot of things at Florent, and I'm not just talking about the food. There are some real philosophers in charge here. Florent is quirky in the best possible way. It's essentially a French coffeeshop, but everyone knows there really isn't such a thing. Or is there?

Breakfast Any Time

Most neighborhood diners will serve you breakfast whenever you want it, but here are some places from this book where you can enjoy breakfast any time:

Amy Ruth's (see page 68) serves its waffles all day until closing.

Balthazar (see page 13) offers a delicious omelette with fries, among other breakfastlike choices, on its late-night menu. Served Monday–Thursday midnight–1 a.m., Friday and Saturday midnight–2 a.m., and Sunday 11 p.m.–midnight.

Florent (see opposite page) serves breakfast 24/7. It also has an excellent breakfast special after 2:30 a.m.: two eggs any style, toast, home fries, juice, and coffee for $7.50. That's probably less than you spent on one drink at the club you just came from.

'ino (see page 39) is doing its part to make Nutella an American staple. You can indulge in a panino made with Nutella, the wonderful hazelnut chocolate spread, every day until 2 a.m.

14. Good Enough to Eat

Just your typical urban neighborhood farmhouse.

❊ BREAKFAST HOURS:

Monday–Friday 8 a.m.–4 p.m.

483 Amsterdam Avenue (between 83rd and 84th streets)

212-496-0163

Upper West Side

www.goodenoughtoeat.com

Good for kids

You're in more than good hands with chef/owner Carrie Levin at Good Enough to Eat. She stays true to classic, American breakfast favorites, and offers appropriately huge portions of what one imagines is served on midwestern farmhouse tables after the chickens are fed and the cows are milked. Thanks to appearances on *Martha Stewart Living*, even my mom in Dallas knows about her spicy turkey sausage, which tastes just like the more fattening stuff. The signature Good Enough to Eat waffles are dense, chewy, and delicious, and the orange butter that they are served with will make you reconsider the need for syrup. The stick-to-your-ribs Irish oatmeal is served simply, with brown sugar and a side of cinnamon toast. The "Farmhouse Breakfast" consists of two poached eggs served over onion dill toast with a side of pork sausage, which are sized somewhere between golf balls and baseballs. The staff is laid-back and the decor is a bright and happy combination of country kitsch and a good sense of humor, with a cow motif throughout.

Good Enough to Eat has been an Upper West Side weekend brunch favorite since 1981. I say skip the block-long weekend brunch lines and enjoy the country charm of this casual breakfast bastion on a special weekday morning when you have time to laze over a cup of coffee and the *New York Times*. On sunny days you can sit out front and watch the slow morning traffic amble up Amsterdam Avenue. It's also a great place for parents with children in tow to get the morning energy fix they need for a trip to the Children's Museum of Manhattan on 83rd Street or the American Museum of Natural History on 81st Street. Without the buzzing weekend crowds, you can sit back and feel like a regular.

15. Home

A true, well, home away from . . .

new york's 50 best places to enjoy breakfast and brunch

❄ BREAKFAST HOURS:

Monday–Friday 9–11:30 a.m.

20 Cornelia Street (between Bleecker and West Fourth streets)

212-243-9579

West Village

www.recipesfromhome.com

Going to Home is as low-key and relaxing as stopping by your best friend's house for breakfast—but can your best friend turn out terrific baked eggs with New York cheddar cheese and grilled homemade salami? The dining room wraps around you like a well-worn quilt, cozy and warm, and the food is just as comforting. When David Page and Barbara Shinn opened the restaurant over ten years ago, they hit on a formula that hasn't stopped working: use local, seasonal ingredients to make simple comfort food. Today, restaurants all over town flaunt their use of local ingredients, but Home was doing it before it became trendy.

The breakfast menu is short and sweet: the basics done well. There are a few surprises—like the toasted breakfast pear cake with honey cream cheese—but mostly you go to Home for familiar fare. Definitely try the great sage sausage from Faicco, a famous pork shop just a couple of blocks away on Bleecker Street, or the perfectly salty, not-too-fatty home-made salami. The oatmeal is stick-to-your-ribs good and the French toast with apple syrup is sweet and satisfying. Home is not a place to grab a quick meal; this is a place for poring over the paper and chatting with your waitperson—or your best friend, who most likely can't cook like the staff at Home.

16. 'ino

A stamp-size charmer for great breakfast sandwiches.

❖ BREAKFAST HOURS:

Monday–Friday 9–11 a.m.

21 Bedford Street (between Downing Street and Sixth
Avenue)

212-989-5769

West Village

www.cafeino.com

You'll wonder how 'ino packs so much great cooking into such
a tiny kitchen when the truffled egg toast is placed in front of
you. The light, white bread and egg drizzled with truffle oil is
a real masterpiece. It's one of those perfect dishes that comes
to mind when thinking about your dream breakfast.

The story goes like this: owners Jason Denton (a part owner
of the fabulous Italian joint Lupa) and Jennifer Denton fell in love
with a little wine bar in Italy. When they returned to New York,
they opened 'ino, a charming little restaurant with Bellini-colored
walls, scrumptious panini, and an excellent breakfast. They've
only got twenty-five seats, but it's well worth the squeeze.

Wonderful coffee drinks are made in a shining, silver behemoth of an espresso machine behind the counter. The egg and
fontina bruschetta is rich and fulfilling on its own, but it's even
better if you add either the crunchy asparagus or salty pancetta.
The Pullman bread from Blue Ribbon Bakery is doughy and well
suited to a slathering of Nutella. (In my opinion Nutella is the
best breakfast spread ever. What could be better than hazelnut
and chocolate? I first had it during a high school trip to Italy, and
ever since, I have admired Italians for figuring out a way to have
chocolate for breakfast.) As you wash that Nutella down with a
piping hot demitasse of espresso, you'll begin to believe the old
adage that good things come in small packages.

17. Kitchenette

It's like having your mom make you breakfast—without the nagging.

✳ BREAKFAST HOURS:
Monday–Friday 7:30 a.m.–4:30 p.m.

1272 Amsterdam Avenue (between 122nd and 123rd streets)
212-531-7600
Morningside Heights

80 West Broadway (at Warren Street)
212-267-6740
Tribeca

Good for kids

Enjoy a taste of the South at Kitchenette. You can easily imagine an early-morning crowd of sheriffs and farmers stopping in for the "Kitchenette Special": two eggs, bacon, and cheese on a biscuit. Kitchenette is also a decidedly New York take on that southern café, because you can just as easily imagine a crowd of yoga instructors and freelance writers stopping in for the "Kitchenless": egg whites, grilled tomato, and smoked turkey on a biscuit.

Both downtown and uptown, these cute-as-a-white-washed-fence spots boast a menu that nicely balances light and heavy comfort classics. "Hole in the Bread" is made with challah toast, which is a great choice to surround the drippy eggs. There is also the "Lumberjack," with two eggs, bacon or turkey sausage (balance, balance), and two plain or fruited pancakes, and the "Farmhouse," with two eggs and a biscuit. (Apparently lumberjacks like pancakes, farmers like biscuits.)

Egg dishes are served with either potatoes or cheese grits. I say go with the grits: they aren't too cheesy, but a nice savory side to mush around with eggs (the way I like them). This is also an extremely kid-friendly place if you can hit it when there isn't a big crowd; otherwise things can feel a little cramped.

One last reason to go to Kitchenette: when I first moved to New York, I received many a strange look when I slathered my eggs with ketchup and Tabasco. When I asked for my condiments at Kitchenette, the waitperson brought both and said, "You're right, they're better that way." And, well, I love to be right.

18. Kittichai

Super-cool space for a Thai-touched breakfast.

❊ BREAKFAST HOURS:
Monday–Sunday 7–11 a.m.
60 Thompson Hotel
60 Thompson Street (between Spring and Broome streets)
212-219-2000
SoHo
Good for business meetings

Chef Ian Chalermkittichai, who lent the second half of his name to the restaurant, was executive chef at the Spice Market restaurant (no relation to Jean-Georges's Manhattan restaurant of the same name) in Bangkok at the Four Seasons. He now presides over this chic eatery in another swanky hotel, the 60 Thompson. The hotel's sultry atmosphere extends to the restaurant's dining room, where the flattering light gives everyone a flawless complexion. The reflecting pool in the center of the room adds to the sexy ambiance at night, but is soothing and relaxing during the day.

Moving on to the menu. Everything I tried at Kittichai was good, but since there are so few places where you can have a Thai-influenced breakfast, I recommend taking advantage of the restaurant's signature cuisine. The Thai coffee is far superior to the cloying versions served at many of the Thai dives around the city. Here it is served either hot or cold, and is tasty either way. One of the most exceptional starters is far from exotic: natural goat's milk yogurt with Chiang Mai honey and berries. The honey is from Thailand, and has floral notes that give this simple dish a special kick. When it comes to ordering your entree, definitely go with the "Kittichai Breakfast Tray," which comes with fried rice with chicken, a soft omelette with a mild Thai flavor, clear soup, and Thai tea. The unexpected combination of the textures and Southeast Asian spices on the tray make for an unusual but truly satisfying morning meal, and the kick from the flavors will perk you up just as much as any caffeine-laden beverage.

Juice It Up!

Sometimes you just don't have time for breakfast, but that shouldn't keep you from enjoying it. Scarfing a bagel on the subway may be the method of choice for many commuters, but there is another way. Over the past few years, the city has seen the installation of two major juice fixtures: Jamba Juice and Juice Generation.

Jamba Juice began, not surprisingly, in California. It is a purveyor of some mighty tasty, mighty healthy juice concoctions, like "Bright Eyed and Blueberry," a creamy, antioxidant-rich delight made from blueberries, strawberries, soy milk, and frozen yogurt, and the "Tropical Awakening," which is a rousing combination of pineapple juice, bananas, strawberries, blueberries, and a creamy dairy base. Each comes with a complimentary "boost"—an add-in that gives your drink a personalized nutritional kick, like the "performance boost," which combines vitamin C, magnesium, and joint-strengtheners chondroitin and glucosamine. Though Jamba Juice's popularity sometimes results in long morning lines, the smoothies are still quicker than the average sit-down breakfast, and often just as healthy.

Juice Generation, a New York native, hocks similar smoothies, with a greater emphasis on health benefits. The smoothies at Juice Generation already contain the add-ins, and the names tell you what they're good for,

19. Kum Gang San

At this 24/7 restaurant, hae jang gook—a traditional Korean breakfast soup—can brighten your morning at 3 a.m. or 10 a.m.

❄ BREAKFAST HOURS:

Monday–Sunday, 24 hours

49 West 32nd Street (between Broadway and Fifth Avenue)

212-967-0909

Garment District

If you wander into Kum Gang San at four in the morning and have to rub at your beer goggles before you realize the mountain range with waterfall is fake, then this all-night Korean joint is just what you need. The super-spicy dishes will sober you right up and keep you from singing along with the renditions of pop classics coming from the white baby grand piano. For the rest of you, Kum Gang San is a terrific place to explore Korean (and some Japanese) cuisine at any time of the day—even for breakfast.

Though only one menu item is denoted as a breakfast dish, any of the options here can help you start your day right. The breakfast soup, *hae jang gook*, is worth waking up (or waiting up all night) for. Described as "traditional Korean morning soup consisting of beef, bean sprouts, Chinese cabbage, green onions in mildly spicy sauce," it isn't as fiery as some of the dishes on the menu, but it will definitely give your morning a kick (but tripe-haters beware). A few years ago, the *New York Times's* Eric Asimov wrote that their hae jang gook "would make a fine winter restorative." I couldn't agree more.

If morning soup isn't your cup of tea, there are a whole host of other options. You can opt for barbecues prepared at the table, for instance, or choose from a wide array of sushi. Still, in the middle of the night or early in the morning, the warm soups and stews call. The seductive and mellow *surlong tang* is an enticing beef and bone marrow soup with hearty noodles and tender pieces of brisket. Kimchi, the pickled cabbage synonymous with Korean cuisine, makes an appearance in a few of the dishes. Its peculiar pungency makes it one of those love-it-or-hate-it tastes, but I fall in the former category and think Kum Gang San's kimchi is delicious. Little side dishes, or *banchan,* accompany every meal, and, in addition to the kimchi, include other Korean favorites like tasty barbecue, a myriad of noodle dishes, and sometimes an odditiy or two like sea urchin. (Vegetarians beware—nothing seemed truly meat-free.)

Kum Gang San is an adventure. One of the great things about New York is that you don't need a passport to get to Korea—just a MetroCard and your appetite.

20. Le Pain Quotidien

They're popping up everywhere, making for tastier mornings all around Manhattan.

❋ BREAKFAST HOURS:
Usually from 7:30 a.m.–closing, but hours and opening times vary by location.

1336 First Avenue (at 72nd Street)
212-717-4800
Upper East Side

922 Seventh Avenue (at 58th Street)
212-757-0775
Midtown

833 Lexington Avenue (at 64th Street)
212-755-5810
Upper East Side

100 Grand Street (at Mercer Street)
212-625-9009
SoHo

1131 Madison Avenue (at 84th Street)
212-327-4900
Upper East Side

50 West 72nd Street (at Columbus Avenue)
212-712-9700
Upper West Side

38 East 19th Street (at Broadway in ABC Carpet & Home)

212-673-7900

Flatiron

www.lepainquotidien.com

Good for kids and leisurely paper reading

I discovered Le Pain Quotidien on my honeymoon in Paris. Early one morning, my husband and I went to a coin-operated laundromat a few blocks from the Louvre. (I love Paris!) While I was watching our skivvies spin, my husband went a few doors down and came back with perfect croissants and divine cafés au lait from a branch of the Belgian-born bakery café, Le Pain Quotidien. When we returned from that trip, we tried the branch on 72nd Street, and unlike many European imports, it was just as good over here. Since then, I've tried branches all over the city, and rest assured, all are equally delicious.

The cornerstone of Le Pain Quotidien is the food it's named for: the daily bread. This is not a café for the carb-conscious. Even the decor pays homage to the bakery, with menus stuck in crusty loaves along the communal farmhouse tables and at the smaller tables. Their croissants are awe-inspiring and the hazelnut and raisin breads are dense and flavorful enough to eat unadorned. Stop by the pastry case if you're in the mood for sweets; the fruit tarts are especially wonderful. Cafés au lait come in big white porcelain bowls perfect for dunking pieces of crusty baguette. The parfait with crunchy, nutty granola and yogurt is served in a tall soda-fountain glass with a long teaspoon for eating. The home-made hazelnut spread doesn't cede ground to chocolate like its close cousin Nutella; it is more like the rich relation of your favorite creamy peanut butter. The rest of the menu is fairly basic with an emphasis on fresh, organic ingredients. Don't limit yourself to the obvious breakfast choices, because I thought the curried chicken salad made a great protein-packed morning repast, as would any of the sandwiches or salads.

Le Pain Quotidien is a great place for kids. I don't know if I've ever met a child who wouldn't want a chocolate croissant for breakfast. To be honest, I don't know an adult who wouldn't feel the same.

Go to Le Pain Quotidien and you'll be eating just what they're eating in France—and Italy, and Belgium, and Los Angeles . . .

21. Mark's

Breakfast never felt so civilized.

❊ BREAKFAST HOURS:

Monday–Sunday 7–10:30 a.m.

The Mark Hotel

25 East 77th Street (between Fifth and Madison avenues)

212-879-1864

Upper East Side

www.mandarinoriental.com

Good for business meetings

When you walk into the dining room at Mark's, you will feel civilized in an Edith Wharton kind of way. Take, for instance, the buffet. This isn't a buffet in the fashion of American gluttony; instead, a discreet table near the entrance is laden with pastries from Balthazar Bakery and freshly cut fruit. Mark's has somehow made self-serve food seem delicate—even refined. The gracious maître d' and the luxuriously cushioned seats serve as additional reminders that refinement can be friendly and comfortable.

The menu features standard breakfast fare, with a few nods toward the calorie-conscious. There are, however, a couple of decadent choices worth mentioning. First, the soft scrambled eggs with black truffles and mascarpone cheese. The earthiness of the truffles is perfectly matched with the fluffy richness of the eggs and taken to heavenly heights with the addition of the creamy mascarpone cheese. Then there is a well-to-do version of steak and eggs, made with a black angus filet mignon, and served with a portion of lip-smacking breakfast potatoes. "The American" is also an excellent choice, with fresh-squeezed juice, two eggs, toast, and a choice of honey-cured ham, apple-smoked chicken sausage, or bacon. Make sure that someone at your table orders the toast. It is served in a traditional metal toast rack, complete with a quilted cozy that sits like a fez on your bread keeping it, well, toasty. For one of the lighter choices, try the sliced papaya with lime and mint. The acidity of the lime is an appropriate companion for the soft sweetness of the papaya.

The service at Mark's is attentive but not overbearing. The dining room is tasseled and upholstered in a style that's a cross between a London men's club and a Parisian sitting room fit to host a lively salon. One morning, a large table to our left was occupied by a group of fiction writers talking about selling their novels to Hollywood, while to our right was a couple talking about how they'd like to leave their Hollywood jobs for a bohemian life in New York. Despite their difference in locational taste, both parties appreciated the privilege of a delicious breakfast at Mark's.

22. Michael's New York

Where minted media deals are as fresh as the fruit and yogurt.

❄ BREAKFAST HOURS:

Monday–Friday 7:30–9:30 a.m.

24 West 55th Street (between Fifth and Sixth avenues)

212-767-0555

Midtown

www.michaelsnewyork.com

Good for business meetings

Business meetings are no longer confined to our offices, and power lunches are a must for the go-getter. But for those who are a step beyond overachiever, there's Michael's. Michael's does a breakfast that will keep your eyes open, even through the dullest morning meeting.

Appropriately situated in the heart of Midtown, Michael's is often mentioned in the society pages as a place where media moguls get things done before many of us have blow-dried our hair. The original Michael's was opened by Michael McCarty in Santa Monica more than twenty-five years ago. In 1994, he introduced his bit of Southern California to Manhattan. The airy, spacious dining room is decorated with paintings by David Hockney, Jasper Johns, and Michael's wife, Jan McCarty.

The cuisine also nods toward our western frontier. The menu begins with a wide selection of fruit choices, and everything I tried was fresh and ripe—a rarity at most breakfast haunts. You can make a nice modest meal with the pastry selection and a small bowl of fruit. If you opt for the breakfast menu, Michael's will either reward you for having some fruit with great brioche French toast, or allow you to stick to your "diet" with an egg-white omelette that has leeks, tomatoes, and mushrooms. The mushrooms are hearty enough to help you ignore that craving for breakfast meats, but if you can't resist, the restaurant has great chicken-apple sausage. The juice is, of course, fresh-squeezed and refreshing. At the end of the menu is this obliging statement: "All items can be modified to accommodate your dietary needs." Can they make blueberry pancakes that won't go to my thighs? I bet they'd try.

Oh, and don't forget to check out the Dennis Hopper photographs in the rest rooms.

23. Pastis

Where to go to see and be seen, and for great classic break-fast dishes.

❉ BREAKFAST HOURS:

Monday–Sunday 9 a.m.–noon

9 Ninth Avenue (at Little West 12th Street)

212-679-2551

Meatpacking District

www.pastisny.com

Good for leisurely paper reading

When I was at Pastis, Julianne Moore was enjoying breakfast with a handsome toddler. Nobody bothered her (as nobody should), so there we were: the very famous and not-so-famous in perfect harmony, sipping coffee in a café that makes you feel very welcome, very New York, and very vacation-in-Provence all at once. *Bienvenue*!

Pastis is a sibling of Balthazar, another offspring of restaurateur Keith McNally. You can see the family resem-blance in its uncanny ability to remain a favorite among the famous long past the shelf-life of most hip spots, and the careful attention it pays to honoring the authenticity of its French inspiration. But where Balthazar is warm and dark, Pastis is lighter and airier, thanks to the tables on the street that extend the long dining room out onto Ninth Avenue. If it's a warm day, sitting outside with your paper watching the very hip troll around the Meatpacking District can be quite a treat. Traffic on Ninth Avenue at this spot is not so bad, and the boxes of lovely flowers create a barrier between diners and the street.

The breakfast menu at Pastis is not extensive, but it more than satisfies, with a well-chosen arsenal of standards that are given a little extra *joie de vivre* from the deft kitchen staff. The fluffy omelette with fine herbs is subtly laced with chives and thyme, giving the dish more complexity than its standard diner counterpart. The Irish oatmeal with sautéed bananas is toothsome, the bananas providing all the sweetness you need; with a little cream, you've got a great way to warm up on a cold fall morning. The pastry selections from Balthazar Bakery are a revelation. The croissants are impossibly flaky, the brioche is light as air, and the pain au chocolat uses bittersweet chocolate to balance the buttery pastry. Top off your meal with a bowl of café au lait for you and a chocolat chaud for your toddler and you're in business—well, in McNally's business, which is a pretty great place to be in the morning.

24. Teresa's

These excellent Polish diners put the "stick-to-your-ribs"
back in breakfast.

❊ BREAKFAST HOURS:
Sunday–Thursday, 7 a.m.–11 p.m., Friday and Saturday
7 a.m.–12 a.m.
103 First Avenue (between Sixth and Seventh streets)
212-228-0604
East Village

80 Montague Street (at Hicks Street)
718-797-3996
Brooklyn Heights
Good for kids

For more than a decade, Teresa Brzozowska's two no-frills coffee shops have been serving the basic coffee shop breakfast, which is quite good, but what she can do with a blintz and pierogi will make you wish you lived around the corner. Let me get the decor out of the way so we can move on to the more important matters at hand: It's cleaner and nicer than most New York City coffee shops, but nothing to write home about. Teresa's is a coffee shop, and it doesn't pretend to be anything more.

Okay, now on to the *raison d'etre* of Teresa's. Since Ratner's closed I've been on a quest for the perfect blintz, and I think we've got a winner. Teresa's crispy-edged pancake acts like a warm blanket for the filling. I think that the version with plum butter is best. The plum butter is an excellent sweet-tart sidekick for the creamy pot-cheese filling. The pierogi are dense and chewy, and there are many filling options, so try a combination. They're all good. It may not sound like regular breakfast fare, but trust me, it should be. The kielbasa that comes with many of the egg dishes isn't too fatty and is just salty enough. One of the great things about Teresa's menu is that many of these dishes come as side orders, so you can piece together an authentic Polish smorgasbord and not miss out on any of these Eastern European treats. Just promise yourself you'll walk home the long way or spend an extra year at the gym. It's worth it.

25. 'wichcraft

Breakfast sandwiches that are downright spellbinding.

❄ BREAKFAST HOURS:

Monday–Friday 8 a.m.–6 p.m.

Saturday and Sunday 10 a.m.–6 p.m.

49 East 19th Street (between Broadway and Park Avenue
South)

212-780-0577

Flatiron

397 Greenwich Street (at Beach Street)

866-942-4272

Chinatown

www.wichcraftny.com

Good for kids and to-go breakfasts

I wish I lived on 19th Street between Broadway and Park
Avenue South. To be honest, I wish I lived surrounded by the
pastry-cream-colored walls with bright orange accents and
surprisingly warm industrial decor that make 'wichcraft so
inviting. Each morning I would be able to choose between
the fried egg, frisée, bacon, and gorgonzola on ciabatta, or
the smoked ham, avocado, and butter on a baguette. I'd hear
them call my name when it was ready (they'll do this for you
too, it's their system) and roll off of my cot in the balcony seating area and pad down the stairs to retrieve my perfect breakfast sandwich.

Tom Colicchio knows the magic of high-quality ingredients. Those of you who have been to Craft, Craftbar, or
Gramercy Tavern know the genius of Colicchio's cooking, as
he is executive chef at all three lauded establishments. At this
sandwich mecca, he applies his culinary smarts to breads and

spreads. His sandwiches aren't fussy, rather they emphasize creative combinations of high-quality ingredients. The fried egg sandwich is a tribute to a classic French frisée salad, of lardons and a poached egg. In Colicchio's sandwich, the crispy slab bacon and runny fried egg coat the frisée, and are given a little kick from the pungent gorgonzola spread on the crusty ciabatta. The onion frittata on a roll with cheddar cheese is rich and earthy. The white cheddar is sharp but the caramelized onions balance the sandwich with their sweetness. The chunky peanut butter with jelly is nothing like what was once packed in your lunchbox; the seasonal flavored jelly puts the jarred stuff to shame. (Cross your fingers for rhubarb.)

Note to dieters: there's nothing for you here. Even the non-sandwich choices are carbo-loaded: buttery scones, a devilish brioche cinnamon roll, steel-cut oatmeal. But if you're going to cheat, this is the place to do it. These are magical sandwiches that can only be the result of some potent 'wichcraft.

Coffee Cart Convenience

New York is the city of convenience. You don't need a car to get around. You can have someone pick up your laundry in the morning and return it, cleaned and folded, in the evening. You can order any meal of the day to be delivered. Someone will even take your dog out for a walk. So of course the Big Apple has its own system of breakfast convenience: the corner coffee cart. On many corners of this fair city, a friendly purveyor can make your coffee just the way you like it, and sell you a bran muffin during bikini season or a doughnut in the heart of winter. Many New Yorkers are loyal to their particular cart; that's why there can be two carts within ten feet of each other, both doing good business. And these carts offer pretty much the best breakfast deal around: a bagel for fifty cents, and a cup of coffee for the same.

There are two carts that have gained notoriety far beyond their humble corners: the **Mud Trucks** have been pouring perfect lattes for their adoring customers for over four years. The bright orange trucks, with their sixties-throwback logos, can brighten your morning with espresso drinks that will give you a caffeine jolt with just a whiff of their steam. But these still are bona fide coffee carts: their "gourmet street coffee" sells at prices a bit lower than the Starbucks the Astor Place cart faces.

Astor Place: Monday–Friday 7 a.m.–5 p.m.
Wall Street: Monday–Friday 7:30 a.m.–5:30 p.m.
www.themudtruck.com

brunch

the joy of brunching

The word "brunch" was supposedly coined in England in 1895 by Mr. Guy Berringer. Mr. Berringer wrote an article titled "Brunch: A Plea" for the now-defunct *Hunter's Weekly*. Mr. Berringer asserted that combining breakfast and lunch on a Sunday morning would allow for Saturday night revelries to last longer and Sundays to be more leisurely. "Brunch is cheerful, sociable, and inciting," the astute Mr. Berringer wrote. "It is talk-compelling. It puts you in a good temper, it makes you satisfied with yourself and your fellow beings, it sweeps away the worries and cobwebs of the week." These words still ring true over one hundred years later. Today, brunch in New York City encompasses any meal eaten before 4 p.m. on a Saturday or a Sunday.

Here in the city that supposedly never sleeps, many Friday and Saturday nights turn into Saturday and Sunday mornings before you've taken off your dancing shoes and tucked yourself into bed. Brunch is a meal that lets you have your pancakes, and sleep until noon too. A hearty midday repast is a great way to shake off a hard night or stressful workweek. It is also good for those of us who go to bed at a reasonable hour and have the energy to socialize early in the day. The leisurely pace of brunch provides the perfect venue for catching up with a group of old friends, or for lingering with a love, gazing into one another's eyes for ridiculously long periods of time. And let's not forget, there are plenty of celebrations that are made more festive by Bloody Marys and mimosas: Father's Day, Mother's Day, and birthdays, to name a few. Many weddings now include a Sunday morning brunch for out-of-town guests. However you include brunch in the fabric of your life, it is one of those meals that should always be joyful. After all, with brunch you can eat, drink, be merry—and still have the rest of the day to enjoy when you're done. Hats off to Mr. Berringer. We're all better off with a little brunch (or a big brunch) in our lives.

Three Royal Dishes (and the castles that serve them)

My doctor says that the best way to keep fit is to "eat breakfast like a king, lunch like a prince, and dinner like a pauper." By my estimation, that means brunch is eating for the whole royal family. Brunch is a meal where dessert can be your main course; alcohol isn't just offered, it's included; and you can throw all caution to the wind and "go for it" gastronomically. The following is a list of the three most decadent and delicious brunch-only dishes to be found in the city. So, don't be shy—you've worked hard all week, you deserve a treat. Just don't forget to wear pants with an elastic waist.

The King

"Wa-Za?"
at Norma's
Le Parker Meridien Hotel
118 West 57th Street (between Fifth and Sixth avenues)
212-708-7460
Midtown
www.parkermeridien.com

The "Wa-Za?" ought to come to your table announced by a flourish of trumpets. If you don't start smiling the second the plate is placed in front of you, well, I think you may be humorless. The "Wa-Za?" is a Belgian waffle on steroids, a galette of thinly sliced bananas over a perfectly cooked waffle stuffed with fresh fruit. The size-of-your-face waffle is smothered with a creamy fruit sauce and then given a crunchy brûlee top. Yes, it's sweet, but it isn't cloying. The waffle is massive enough to balance the fruity sweetness of its accompaniments, so it won't put you in a sugar coma. All hail the king of decadent brunch treats!

The Queen

Rolled omelette soufflé
at Ouest
2315 Broadway (at 84th Street)
212-580-8700
Upper West Side
www.ouestny.com

What is a rolled omelette soufflé? Imagine the lightest, fluffiest omelette you can, and then puff it up like a soufflé. Now, stuff that omelette/soufflé with spinach and gruyere cheese . . . The description of this royally delicious dish doesn't even begin to do it justice. Eggs taken to heavenly heights—that's what a rolled omelette soufflé is. The spinach seems to have been blown dry by hand, as none of the typical wateriness of eggs cooked with spinach is seen here. The nutty gruyere cheese, which is the ultimate Swiss cheese, melds seamlessly with the eggs and spinach. The combination of delightful textures and flavors will have you raising your mimosa to toast the queen of indulgent brunch dishes.

The Prince

Spicy chicken with sweet potato hash
at Mesa Grill

102 Fifth Avenue (between 15th and 16th streets)

212-807-7400

Union Square

www.mesagrill.com

Bobby Flay's spicy chicken with sweet potato hash is a brunch dish that combines the regal air of Prince William with the mischievousness of Prince Harry. Inspired by a classic eggs Benedict, here pristine poached eggs rest atop spicy chicken with sweet potato hash, covered with a green chile hollandaise. The green chiles cut the typically rich hollandaise and wake up every bite you take. The hash is chunky and spicy, an ideal foil for the smooth textures of the rest of the dish. The moist chicken, with its southwestern kick, is tempered by the sweet potatoes' earthy sugariness. This brunch dish is clearly in line for the throne.

1. Aix

Go to Provence, sans jet lag.

❈ BRUNCH HOURS:
Sunday 11:30 a.m.–2:30 p.m.
2398 Broadway (at 88th Street)
212-874-7400
Upper West Side
www.aixnyc.com
Good for celebrations

For years, the Upper West Side was a kind of culinary no-man's-land: nothing good ever survived. But recently, a few brave chefs have staked out some turf and are turning culinary desolation into a culinary destination. One of your first stops on an Upper West Side epicurean adventure should be Aix, Didier Virot's happy tribute to Provence. The restaurant's decor of the signature Provençal cornflower blue and saffron yellow immediately transports you to the charming university town for which the restaurant is named. The space is large enough to give you elbow room, but through warm lighting and architectural detail has managed to retain a feeling of intimacy. The service at Aix is a congenial combination of breezy and attentive; your waitperson is both a friendly guide and unassuming server. This is one of those places where you can have a formal Mother's Day brunch, or enjoy an impromptu meal before a visit to the American Museum of Natural History or a stroll in the park on a nice day.

Virot was previously executive chef at Jean Georges, so it should come as no surprise that everything on the French-accented brunch menu is superb. The brunch at Aix features standard fare with French accents. The prix fixe ($25) starts with either a Bloody Mary or *bien mûre*, a delicious concoction of champagne, blackberry puree, and blackberry liqueur.

Main courses include the eggs Provençal, a plate of poached eggs with soft polenta, tomato *concassé*, and basil and Parmesan cheese. The soft polenta is a perfect bed for the poached eggs, and when both elements are melded together on your plate, the flavors sing in delightful harmony. Another excellent choice is the smoked salmon, thin slices of buttery salmon presented with cucumber, grainy mustard, cream cheese, and toasted brioche. The addition of mustard to this classic dish is surprisingly good. The prix fixe ends with your choice of a banana split or a dreamy soufflé with hazelnut-peanut-butter ice cream. There are many a la carte options, including the out-of-this-world hangar steak with *béarnaise* and French fries. Aix also has an excellent wine list, either as an elegant hair-of-the-dog antidote or a way to deal with the family celebration that you were smart to stage at this comfortable but chic establishment.

2. Amy Ruth's

A Harlem haven for heavenly soul food.

❄ BRUNCH HOURS:

Monday–Sunday, 24 hours

113 West 116th Street (between Lenox and Seventh
avenues)

212-280-8779

Harlem

www.amyruthsrestaurant.com

Good for kids

If you've ever wondered why it's called "soul food," the offerings at Amy Ruth's will clarify things perfectly. Amy Ruth's
southern cooking makes you feel warmed, uplifted, com-
forted, and all the other things that you need to nourish your
soul. Named for the grandmother of chef/owner Carl Red-
ding, Amy Ruth's is open seven days a week, but I include it
as a brunch destination because the portions are huge, and
the best dishes on the menu shouldn't be followed by a day
of work; instead, they should be followed by a nap, a trip to
the gym, and maybe a lymphatic massage (not necessarily in
that order).

After you are seated at this perennially bustling spot,
turn your attention to the waffle section of the menu. The
"Reverend Al Sharpton" waffles are at the top of the list for
good reason: they should be ordered immediately, without
hesitation. The giant, crisp waffle is served with either fried
chicken or smothered chicken (fried chicken smothered in
creamy gravy). Nothing beats chicken and waffles done right,
and Amy Ruth's hits the nail on the head with this outstanding
dish. The waffle choices are endless, some savory, some
sweet, but all of them will make you loosen your belt before
you sink into that last bite. Also outstanding are the

smothered pork chops, meaty and just spicy enough to counter the thick gravy, and best when accompanied by the slow-cooked collard greens. Amy Ruth's has a great children's menu, and it even has a few vegan and vegetarian choices.

A trip to Amy Ruth's is worth every calorie (and there are a lot to be had here!). After you're done with your meal, walk six blocks south to the north entrance of Central Park. This is one of the nicest sections of the park, with the Conservatory Gardens and Harlem Meer. Besides, you'll probably feel better if you walk off at least a few of those delightfully acquired chicken-and-waffle calories.

3. Aquagrill

This fish spot makes a swimmingly good brunch.

❄ BRUNCH HOURS:

Saturday and Sunday noon–3:45 p.m.

210 Spring Street (at Sixth Avenue)

212-274-0505

SoHo

Good for celebrations

Aquagrill is an unassuming little spot on a corner of Sixth Avenue, right by where the traffic feeds into the Holland Tunnel. What lurks inside this bright, ocean-blue address is an innovative seafood restaurant with an unbeatable oyster bar, excellent service, and an exciting brunch menu.

Start with the oysters. There's a wonderful feeling of decadence that accompanies sipping a mimosa while eating your freshly shucked oyster—one that has been splashed with a spoonful of savory *mignonette* sauce—during the daylight hours. (If you aren't bivalve savvy, the waitperson will happily guide you through your choices.)

This is a place to listen closely to the specials, because they are inspired by the day's available seafood. On one of my visits, hamachi tuna with ginger soy sauce and edamame eggplant was a special; it was out of this world. The preparation was simple and the flavors melded together like a dream. The set appetizers are also tempting. The warm octopus salad is a real winner, with roasted red peppers, peppercress (think spicier watercress), and roasted onion vinaigrette. When you move on to entrees, there are a few choices that don't feature seafood. They're all tasty, but Aquagrill is all about its innovative takes on the fruits of the sea. There is a good reason that the signature, much-written-about dish is the grilled Atlantic salmon with a falafel crust, cucumbers, and tomatoes in a lemon coriander vinaigrette. The salmon is meaty enough to handle the rustic Mediterranean flair of the crust. The crab Benedict is beyond compare. The sweetness of the fresh Maine peekytoe crabmeat is a perfect replacement for the traditional Canadian bacon. There's so much to love on the Aquagrill menu, and the staff is eager to please, always able to explain preparations and to make suggestions for complementary dishes.

If it's a warm day, sit outside on the small deck overlooking the street. The impeccable service, the delicious food, and the pretty flower boxes will make Sixth Avenue disappear. If the aforementioned combination doesn't completely transport, the fabulous wine list and the special brunch libations will whisk you away.

4. Aquavit

Who'd have thought a Swedish smorgasbord could be so elegant?

❄ BRUNCH HOURS:

Sunday noon–2:30 p.m.

65 East 55th Street (between Madison and Park avenues)

212-307-7311

Midtown

www.aquavit.org

Good for celebrations

Note: Although jackets are not required for brunch, the restaurant does encourage "business casual" dress (no jeans).

In January 2005, after seventeen years on West 54th Street, Swedish-born chef Marcus Samuelsson moved his famous Aquavit to new digs on East 55th. Though Aquavit is known for Nordic delicacies, the sleek, modern, Scandinavian decor is far from cold. The warm lighting and gracious service turns a Sunday brunch into an elegant adventure.

Aquavit serves a prix-fixe brunch buffet—but this is nothing like the typical American kind. Aquavit serves a plentiful smorgasbord, but don't be put off by the image of stuffing yourself until you can't breathe that the American use of this term connotes. As the menu instructs, you don't need to have one of everything. The menu's page of instructions, titled "How best to enjoy the Aquavit smorgasbord," also recommends spacing things out in approximately four courses. (Apart from that, the brunch menu only lists the drinks, including a fabulous signature Bloody Mary made with the house horseradish-infused *aquavit*, the traditional Scandinavian liquor.) Even if you're a rule breaker, trust the instructions; you'll be justly rewarded.

Start with the herrings. There are at least four different kinds, from a traditional creamed herring to a more adventurous curry-based dish. Don't be afraid—all of Samuelsson's preparations are fresh and delicious. After the herring, you'll likely move on to the different preparations of cured salmon—the flavors here probably bear no resemblance to anything you've ever put on a bagel. Then you'll move on to the warm dishes, which include braised meats and Swedish meatballs that a cafeteria lunch lady would never recognize. Finally, there are divine desserts, with enough choices to please any palate, from assortments of fresh fruits to a flaky apple-strudel–like pastry and wonderfully decadent chocolate concoctions.

After we ate brunch at Aquavit, my dining companion said, "That was so much fun." And he was right: brunch at Aquavit is fun because it's unusual, interactive—and elegant.

5. @SQC

Pick your poison: thirteen decadent hot chocolate concoctions or eight bracing variations on the Bloody Mary.

❊ BRUNCH HOURS:
Saturday and Sunday 10 a.m.–3 p.m.
270 Columbus Avenue (between 72nd and 73rd streets)
212-579-0100
Upper West Side
www.sqcnyc.com

@SQC, named for chef Scott Q. Campbell, is a great place for any kind of brunch, whether you're going to gab with a group of friends or moon over a new lover. The seating is extraordinarily comfy and begs you to linger over your meal.

You'll certainly be inclined to settle in for a while if you start with The "Bodacious Bloody Mary Brunch Bar" menu, which features eight different takes on the classic brunch nip. I was especially keen on the "Spicy Mary" with tomatillo and chipotle; it's smoky, spicy, and a darn good pick-me-up. (See the sidebar opposite for more details on the libations.) If you are in the mood for something a little more innocent (or not, you'll see . . .) check out the "@SQC Seriously Delicious Hot Chocolate Bar" menu, featuring everything from a classic hot chocolate to the more sinful "Rummbled Hot Chocolate" with a shot of Meyer's rum.

Once you've decided on your drink, the rest is a breeze; whatever you choose to accompany your cocktail will be great. The eggs Renata packs in all the basic brunch goodies with an Italian flair. It's a twist on classic bruschetta, with a broiler-toasted piece of baguette topped with oven-roasted tomatoes, fresh mozzarella, two fried eggs, and smoky sausage. The lemon-poppy griddle cakes will satisfy your sweet tooth without overwhelming it. The cakes are eggy with a subtle lemon flavor and tasty fruit compote on top. The crispy potato pancakes are wonderful and are served with the appropriate sour cream and applesauce toppings. (Every year, Campbell cooks up a gourmet Passover seder. The brunch potato pancakes prove how well Campbell knows his way around Jewish food.) For the times when you're not in the mood for a heavy mid-morning meal, @SQC also makes a zesty Caesar salad.

This is a popular brunch spot, so be prepared to wait. If you can, try to grab a seat at the window so that you can watch the morning foot traffic along Columbus Avenue. After you're done, you can walk to the Rose Planetarium and the American Museum of Natural History, or head to Central Park.

Hair of the Dog

The Romans had a saying, *similia simbilibus curantur*, meaning "like things cure like." It was thought that the cure for a dog bite was the burnt hair of the dog that bit you. So to cure that hangover from your Saturday night vodka-martini fest, you should have a Sunday morning Bloody Mary.

Even if you don't believe that adage, why not take advantage of brunch's unique tippling opportunity. Brunch is the only time when drinking before happy hour is actually encouraged. **@SQC** on the Upper West Side (see opposite page) offers eight different variations on the Bloody Mary. These include the "Classy Mary," a tall glass of vodka and tomato juice with visible pieces of fresh horseradish, and the "Guadalupe," with tomato juice, tequila, and fresh lime juice. **Essex** (120 Essex Street at Rivington) has a "Liquid Brunch" prix fixe ($14) that comes with three—yes, three!—make-sure-you-bring-cab-fare-to-get-you-home mimosas, Bloody Marys, or screwdrivers. Rumor has it that the waitstaff lose count before you do and the libations just keep flowing. The waits can be long, but the Latin-American-meets-Eastern-European fare is tasty—but really, after three screwdrivers, who cares?

6. Blue Ribbon Bakery

This West Village brunch mainstay is worth lining up for.

✤ BRUNCH HOURS:
  Saturday and Sunday 11:30 a.m.–4 p.m.
  35 Downing Street (at Bedford Street)
  212-337-0404
  West Village

On a chilly fall morning, my husband and I rounded the corner at Bedford and Downing streets, and saw a crowd. A formidable thirty-person-plus crowd had congregated in front of Blue Ribbon Bakery. It was 11:25 a.m. Guess the Blue Ribbon fans don't sleep in. Through the picture windows, you could see a busy staff finishing up the table preparations. It was one of those moments where you know you're going to have to wait, I mean really wait. My husband looked at me, Sunday *Times* tucked beneath his arm, and said, "This better be good." And you know what? It was.

Blue Ribbon draws a crowd because the service is friendly, the atmosphere is warm and inviting, and above all, the brunch dishes are great. The brunch menu is short and sweet, featuring classics with a twist, like a shrimp and bacon hash. If you've ever had bacon-wrapped shrimp, you know what a delicious combination that can be. Blue Ribbon takes this excellent pairing to another level with the addition of a rich, creamy hollandaise sauce. The challah French toast is also a good choice. The huge rafts of egg-soaked bread are piled high on the plate, and are just the right density to soak up the Vermont maple syrup. The decor is cozy and simple, and don't worry if you are seated downstairs—what you lose in street views you gain in intimate charm.

Blue Ribbon is now a veritable empire. In addition to Blue Ribbon Bakery, Bruce and Eric Bromberg are the proud owners of the **Blue Ribbon** restaurant (on Sullivan Street in SoHo), **Blue Ribbon Sushi** (with Park Slope and SoHo locations), and now, **Blue Ribbon Brooklyn** in Park Slope (which also serves a mean Sunday brunch). Blue Ribbon Brooklyn is located on Fifth Avenue between 1st Street and Garfield Place. This may be your answer to avoiding the Manhattan crowds, but the way things are changing in Park Slope, you may have just as many Brooklynites to contend with in line.

7. Calle Ocho

A little nuevo Latino to spice up your Sunday.

✴ BRUNCH HOURS:

Sunday 11:30 a.m.–3 p.m.

446 Columbus Avenue (between 81st and 82nd streets)

212-873-5025

Upper West Side

Good for celebrations

Named for the bustling 8th Street in Miami's Little Havana, Calle Ocho is an unusually sunny spot among the myriad brunch choices on the Upper West Side. Particularly mood-boosting during the depths of a New York winter, Calle Ocho is a bastion of warmth, thanks to the sun-kissed frescoes on the walls, the smiles from the staff, and the spicy adventure it provides. Get out the sunscreen and put on your sunglasses: This is not your typical Latin restaurant.

You'll need those shades to read the dazzling menu. Start with the *datiles*, almond-stuffed dates wrapped in bacon and served with blue cheese sauce. The mingling of flavors—the sweet dates with the salty bacon and pungent blue cheese—is a three-part marriage made in heaven. The *camarones*, a shrimp ceviche with lime, jalapeño, and lemon oil, is an effervescent dish of incomparable freshness and simplicity. Don't turn up your nose at the *empanadas*, which bear no resemblance to the greasy versions often found at street vendors around town. Calle Ocho's are light and airy with complex spiced fillings. Move on to the *pan de bono* Benedict. Pan de bono are chewy rolls made from *cassava*, a starchy tropical root, and cheese. Here the rolls are topped with chorizo (spicy Spanish sausage) hash, poached eggs, and a hollandaise sauce that has been given a Latin twist with the addition of fragrant cilantro. Each dish is a pleasing amalgam of bold spices and authentic Latin flavors.

If you like libations with your brunch, definitely try one of Calle Ocho's mojitos. The classic preparation is light rum, lime juice, mint, and sugar, but Calle Ocho also serves flavored variations, including the raspberry mojito, which uses a light raspberry-infused rum. Whatever you choose to drink, sip it slowly, because you should savor your time in this oasis. With marimba music playing, a group of good friends, and the exceptional food, you'll be sad when your vacationlike repast has ended. But don't worry: The good thing about Calle Ocho is that you can visit any time.

8. Candle 79

Proving that brunch can be healthy (as well as delicious).

❊ BRUNCH HOURS:

Saturday noon–3:30 p.m.; Sunday noon–4 p.m.

154 East 79th Street (near Lexington Avenue)

212-537-7179

Upper East Side

www.candlecafe.com

Good for vegetarians and vegans

Don't be fooled by the spartan brunch menu at Candle 79—there is nothing meager about the dining experience at this stylish vegetarian haven. Happily, neither are there the hints of stern self-righteousness that pervade the atmosphere at other vegan eateries. Instead, the bi-level restaurant welcomes you with a friendly, bright-eyed staff, and sensuous photos of fruits and vegetables hanging on the walls. The atmosphere downstairs is somewhat casual, with plenty of light pouring through the picture windows that look out on 79th Street; upstairs is slightly more elegant. But both areas have a welcoming, "real restaurant" feel, and will reassure even the most finicky diner that eating your greens can be a gourmet pleasure.

After you are seated, you will be given a postcard-size brunch menu along with the full-size lunch menu. While there are a ton of tasty options on the lunch menu, I encourage you to stick with the brunch choices. You can come any day of the week for lunch, but on the weekends, the kitchen tries its adept vegan hand on some brunch classics. The apple cinnamon pancakes come with a ginger maple syrup that wakes up this hearty item with a pleasantly spicy kick. The brunch burrito is a real winner. Nestled inside a large tortilla wrapper is a portion of seitan ragout, carmelized onions, spinach, brown rice, and spicy chipotle black beans. For those who have been subjected to one-too-many charmless meat substitutes, fear not: this seitan isn't trying to be meat. The texture of this wheat-gluten–based protein is reminiscent of roasted, shredded chicken, but it's a bit softer and adds an unexpected heartiness to the burrito. Served with creamy tofu sour cream, *guajillo* sauce—made from piquant guajillo peppers–and a super-fresh salsa, this is one of the best vegetarian burritos I have ever had. There is also a tofu scramble with seasonal vegetables, served with expertly spiced roasted potatoes and fresh mesculin salad. The sourdough French toast is complemented by pear and cranberry compote. All four of these brunch choices are delicious and filling without weighing you down for the rest of the day. When everything tastes so fantastic, it's easy to forget that it's good for you.

Don't overlook the drinks menu, which includes a "Smooth Sippers" section of delicious concoctions. The "Limeade," made with crushed ice, lemon and lime juices, and agave nectar, is a refreshing, up-market cousin of a slushy. There is also a nice selection of unusual juices, like the "Green Goddess," a surprising blend of mixed greens, apple, lemon, and ginger.

9. Dumonet at the Carlyle

A pinch-me-I'm-dreaming brunch in an equally fabulous setting.

❊ BRUNCH HOURS:

Sunday noon–3 p.m. (specific seating times, call for reservations)

35 East 76th Street (at Madison Avenue)

212-570-7192

Upper East Side

www.thecarlyle.com

Good for special occasions

Note: jacket required

Let me describe my perfect New York City Sunday: waking up late to discover a sunny day, flipping through the Sunday *Times*, having a cup of coffee, then putting on my Sunday best (with some comfy shoes). Then I start walking east through Central Park until I feel a little growl in my stomach, at which point I'm at the Carlyle, where, coincidentally, I have a noon reservation for brunch at Dumonet. Afterward, I'd walk over to the Whitney Museum or the Metropolitan Museum of Art and while away the rest of the day. While this might not be your perfect Sunday, I guarantee that if you include brunch at Dumonet in yours, you will not be sorry.

From the moment you walk into the dining room you'll know you're in a special place. The restaurant is perfectly nestled in the hotel's lobby, and the garden-inspired decor is elegant, with just enough playfulness to keep it from being uncomfortably fancy. If you're there with a significant other, it's romantic to sit side by side at one of the small tables along the banquet that flanks the walls. The delicate glass chandeliers give everyone a soft, healthy glow. The service is impeccable and the food—magnificent. You can choose from the buffet or order a la carte. The buffet has many traditional brunch buffet items, including beautiful salmon, crisp salads, and succulent roasts. The desserts on the buffet are decadent and plentiful—you could satisfy your sweet tooth just by looking. The menu is as rich as the buffet and just as satisfying. (Don't miss the chicken hash with foie gras.) The clientele during the brunch hours is wonderfully continental. One Sunday, my husband and I sat in between tables occupied by visitors speaking Portuguese and French. The waitstaff navigated all of the language barriers with the grace of Olympic hurdlers. The sated look on each diner's face after finishing his or her meal could be universally understood. As we stepped out onto the sunny sidewalk, we felt satisfied and pampered. We felt as if we were having a perfect New York Sunday.

10. Eleven Madison Park

Breezily elegant and serving up surprising twists on brunch classics.

❄ BRUNCH HOURS:

Saturday and Sunday 11:30 a.m.–2 p.m.

11 Madison Avenue (at 24th Street)

212-889-0905

Flatiron

www.elevenmadisonpark.com

Good for celebrations

For those accustomed to modest, homey brunch joints, Eleven Madison Park can be overwhelming. Located in the lobby of the MetLife building, it is, by Manhattan standards, huge. It is a refreshing change of pace from the many New York restaurants that have no choice but to be intimate and charming. That's not to say that Eleven Madison Park is charmless; it just went to a different charm school, one where elbow room and tree-size flower arrangements are illuminated by natural light from floor-to-ceiling windows and the warm glow of wall sconces. The leaf "logo" that covers many of the restaurant surfaces is a dignified nod toward the recently revitalized Madison Square Park, situated just across the street.

Chef Kerry Heffernan's menu offers many items a la carte, and a prix-fixe market menu. I recommend ordering a la carte so that you can enjoy mixing and matching interesting combinations of flavors from the appetizers and main courses. It's fun to share at Eleven Madison Park, because everything is so good. If you're in the mood for something rich, try the foie gras terrine for an appetizer, which is made with beef shank, leeks, foie gras, and Banyuls, a sweet wine from the south of France. The entrees include a delectable smoked salmon soft pretzel, a creative take on the traditional lox and bagels in which a soft pretzel substitutes for the bagel. The pretzel is as chewy as a bagel, but the chunks of salt on its well-done exterior are a solid base for the delicate smoked salmon. If your sweet tooth beckons, go with the cinnamon pumpkin waffles, served with sticky pecans and maple cream. Washed down with the exceptional coffee, these waffles put any diner Belgian waffle to shame.

Eleven Madison Park has two private dining rooms that can be reserved for special occasions. They would be perfect places to celebrate Mother's Day or to host a memorable post-wedding brunch.

11. Five Points

At this downtown brunch favorite, the homey dishes are as soothing as the river that runs through it.

❄ BRUNCH HOURS:

    Sunday 11:30 a.m.–3 p.m.

    31 Great Jones Street (between Lafayette Street and Bowery)

    212-253-0700

    NoHo

    www.fivepointsrestaurant.com

It may not be the first thing that comes to mind when you wake up in the morning, but a BLT is a great brunch dish—especially the flawless one at Five Points. The thick pieces of hand-cut smoked bacon with lettuce and marinated tomatoes on Sullivan Street Bakery bread inspire Proustian memories.

Five Points gets most of its brunch dishes just right. The menu is extensive, specializing in hip takes on traditional comfort foods like macaroni and cheese and buttermilk fried chicken. There are also a number of scrumptious egg dishes for brunch patrons with a hankering for breakfast. A standout: the basted eggs with smokehouse bacon. The sweet dishes are also worth trying. The dulce de leche French toast is thick and rich, but not too cloying. All of the dishes are bolstered by chef Marc Meyers's reliance on locally grown ingredients.

The restaurant itself is extremely pleasant. On warm days, you can sit at one of the sidewalk tables and watch the people stroll by. In the main dining room, there is a wonderful little stream that runs the length of the room. Its sound is soothing, encouraging patrons to relax, enjoy, and take their time—the epitome of a satisfying brunch experience.

After brunch, amble around the corner to the Public Theatre, and see if you can catch a matinee.

12. The Golden Unicorn

Where the dim sum is yum-yum.

❄ BRUNCH HOURS:

Saturday and Sunday 9 a.m.–3 p.m.

18 East Broadway (at Catherine Street)

212-941-0911

Chinatown

Good for larger gatherings and celebrations

Dim sum is the Chinese equivalent of brunch—or at least that's the case in the United States. The Cantonese tradition of serving dim sum has become ubiquitous in restaurants in Chinatown. The problem isn't finding dim sum, it's choosing the best place to have it. Many New Yorkers will argue that their favorite dim sum palace is the best, but the reason I have chosen The Golden Unicorn goes beyond personal taste.

The Golden Unicorn is located in a nondescript office building in the heart of Chinatown. Finding it can be a challenge for those who are not familiar with the maze of streets in this neighborhood. Just keep asking, though, and people on the street will point you in the right direction. When you finally reach the building, you'll realize that your adventure is only beginning. In the lobby, which, during crowded times, is teeming with eager patrons, you'll be given a plastic tag with a number. When your number is called, you'll take one of the elevators to whatever floor you've been assigned.

When the elevator doors to the dining room open, the real fun begins. The red-and-gold-colored dining rooms are a cross between a classic Chinese restaurant and the dining room in an unremarkable chain hotel. The cacophony of voices speaking Chinese, English, and other languages gives the room real energy.

Once you're seated, a waiter will serve drinks and assist

you with condiments, but unless you decide to order off the menu, you'll get your food from the women in paper hats pushing the silver carts around the room (this is the recommended course of action). The metal carts move slowly, each offering a different dish. Some of the dim sum choices are hidden in steamers, so the carts have photos to help guide you. There are dumplings served in bamboo steamers with pork, shrimp, and vegetable fillings; tiny chunks of ribs that you pop into your mouth whole, removing the bone when ready to swallow; banana leaves filled with steamed sticky rice; and the sweet sesame balls, served two to a plate. When the server snips them open to let the steam escape, their plum-butter filling is revealed. There are even more exotic-to-Americans choices like duck web and chicken feet, deep-fried and served in a sauce. Even if you aren't sure about something, it's fun to try all of the dishes you can. On one Sunday, I think we sampled at least ten different items.

Dim sum means "so close to the heart." The Golden Unicorn is a great place to come with a large group, because sharing isn't just encouraged, it's actually the only way to sample the full range of delights offered. So gather that group of those "close to your heart" and share a special culinary experience.

How Do You Take Your Coffee?: A Coffee Drink Primer

Double-half-caf-no-foam-whip-latte. What does it all mean? Is this combination even possible? Read on to find out.

espresso: a brewing method that quickly forces hot water through the grounds, creating a strong brew. The grounds-to-water ratio is much closer to one-to-one than that used in brewing regular coffee.

Americano: a shot of espresso with five to eight ounces of hot water added to dilute the strength. (You can imagine why it was dubbed "Americano.")

breve: the use of steamed half-and-half rather than milk.

café au lait: a one-to-one ratio of coffee and heated milk.

café latte: a one-to-three ratio of espresso to steamed milk.

café macchiato: a shot of espresso with a dollop of steamed milk on top.

cappuccino: an equal ratio of espresso, steamed milk, and frothed milk.

double: two shots of espresso in a drink. (The ratio of other ingredients should remain the same.)

foam: frothed milk.

half-caf: a mixture of half caffeinated, half decaffeinated coffee.

mocha: a latte or cappuccino with a shot of chocolate syrup.

skinny: the use of skim milk rather than whole.

whip: whipped cream on top.

13. Les Halles

Anthony Bourdain does a brasserie brunch.

❋ BRUNCH HOURS:

Saturday and Sunday noon–4 p.m.

411 Park Avenue South (between 28th and 29th streets)

212-679-4111

Flatiron

Les Halles Downtown

15 John Street (between Broadway and Nassau streets)

212-285-8585

Tribeca

www.leshalles.net

If you don't know who Anthony Bourdain is, he'd be surprised. Bourdain gained a reputation as a kitchen *enfant terrible* with a heart of gold with *Kitchen Confidential*, a candid rant about his experiences in the restaurant business. The celebrity factor doesn't taint the simple, classic, delicious food of his midtown brasserie Les Halles, or its sister branch downtown. If come dinnertime you're in the mood for a hangar steak, Les Halles, named for the famed Parisian market district, is the place to go.

It is also an excellent place to enjoy brunch. This is the hearty side of French food that can cure a hangover or truly replace two meals in one sitting. Many of the meats come from Bourdain's butcher shop, next door to the midtown location, and you can sample some at brunch in the excellent steak sandwich. The sandwich of grilled rump steak is served with roasted onions and crunchy *pommes frites*, and it goes very well with a fizzy mimosa or a full-bodied red selected from the excellent wine list. If you're having coffee, try the eggs Benedict. The hollandaise sauce at Les Halles makes that of its innumerable competitors (what brunch place doesn't serve eggs Benedict?) seem amateur. If you've ever made hollandaise at home, you know that it is actually a pretty delicate operation. If left to sit, or with the wrong ratio of ingredients, it can become a gelatinous mess. What you get from Les Halles is a perfectly balanced, not-too-thick, not-too-thin saucy revelation. Also try the Les Halles preparation of *ouefs pochés parisienne*, the wondrous salad of frisée with poached eggs and bacon. The fat from the bacon and the oozing warm yoke of the poached egg make a wonderful dressing for the greens. Bourdain may be a rebel in some ways, but when it comes to French cooking, he follows the rules, and his deference pays off.

14. Maroons

Caribbean food you'll want to be stranded with.

new york's 50 best places to enjoy breakfast and brunch

❄ BRUNCH HOURS:
Saturday and Sunday 11:30 a.m.–3 p.m. (Chelsea)
Sunday 11 a.m–4 p.m. (Harlem)

244 West 16th Street (between Seventh and Eighth
avenues)
212-206-8640
Chelsea

300 West 145th Street (at Bradhurst Avenue)
Phone number not available at time of publication.
Harlem
Note: Sunday brunch at this location is a gospel/jazz
brunch.
www.maroonsnyc.com

There are many good times to go to Maroons, but the best
is in the heart of winter. I'm not talking about one of those
pretty snowy Sundays, when the city is breathtaking. I'm talking about, say, mid-February, when the snow is slushy and
gray, the windchill is in the Antarctic range, and if there were
any justice in the world, you'd be at your vacation home in
Jamaica. Luckily for those of us without the vacation home,
you can get a little taste of Jamaica any time of the year at
Maroons. Though the restaurant is located in Chelsea, the
food can transport you to a sunnier place on even the drea-
riest day.

The brunch dishes at Maroons are hearty soul food items
with a Caribbean flourish. The "Roots Breakfast" is spicy cod-
fish served with *callaloo* (greens) and hearty fried dumplings.
The crispy crust around the juicy meat of "Grandma's fried

chicken" sets this dish apart from the greasy versions served at so many other establishments. You can have your chicken with waffles, grits, or home fries. Each of these side dishes holds its own on the plate with the main event, particularly the thick and satisfying white corn grits that accompany many of the dishes. Sharing at Maroons is encouraged, so take a few friends and enjoy the range of offerings. It'll warm you up so thoroughly that by the time you're done, you may be surprised that you don't have to pass through customs on your way out.

15. Mesa Grill

The southwest shines in the deft hands of Bobby Flay.

❊ BRUNCH HOURS:

Saturday 11:30 a.m.–2:30 p.m., Sunday 11:30 a.m.–3 p.m.

102 Fifth Avenue (between 15th and 16th streets)

212-807-7400

Union Square

www.mesagrill.com

Good for celebrations

Bobby Flay has written cookbooks, fought Iron Chefs (and has become one himself), and has several different cooking shows under his belt. Does his cooking live up to his impressive resume? Yes, it does. Mesa Grill, the more casual of his three New York restaurants (Bolo and Bar Americain are the others), offers fantastic takes on southwestern cuisine. Don't be put off by the restaurant's hyper-cute, eighties Santa Fe decor. As soon as the bread basket is set down in front of you, with its mouthwatering savory and sweet contents—including cheddar biscuits, jalapeño corn muffins, and blueberry coffee cake—you'll have a hard time taking your eyes off the food.

If I had the space, I'd describe everything on the brunch menu. There's something about the southwestern flavors that blends so perfectly with brunch. I'll start with the goat cheese *queso fundido*. Traditional queso fundido is essentially a Mexican version of fondue; here, it is made with a creamy goat cheese. It's out of this world. If you are in the mood for lighter fare, try the spicy tuna tartare, served with *serrano* hot sauce and avocado relish. When you move on to the entrees, you'll be faced with a hard choice. (I've described one dish, the spicy chicken and sweet potato hash, in the "Royal Dishes" section, page 65.) Try the baked eggs and toasted white corn bread with tomatillo salsa and mango-glazed bacon. Yes, mango-glazed bacon. Pork and mangoes make happy bed-fellows. Or there's the huge (and hugely pleasing) Mesa burger with cheddar cheese, grilled vidalia onions, and horse-radish mustard on a roll with spicy fries. If I had the space, I could go on and on about the food for chapters; suffice it to say, it's all terrific.

The service is also excellent. This is a popular spot with tourists, but it doesn't have a touristy vibe. Mesa Grill is always a great spot for brunch, whether you're hosting out-of-town guests or having a small family meal. After you're done, you can saunter over to the Union Square green market and try to identify which ingredients in your meal came from there.

16. Norma's

There's a reason it's the most talked-about brunch spot in town.

❊ BRUNCH HOURS:

> Monday–Friday 6:30 a.m.–3 p.m., Saturday and Sunday
> 7 a.m.–3 p.m.
> Le Parker Meridien Hotel
> 118 West 57th Street (between Fifth and Sixth avenues)
> 212-708-7460
> Midtown
> www.parkermeridien.com
> Good for celebrations
> Note: reservations can be hard to get.

Norma's doesn't serve dinner and it doesn't even really serve lunch, although you can eat there during lunch hours. Norma's—happy sigh—is simply a temple dedicated to the worship of the morning meal. If you've ever visited the refined Le Parker Meridien, you may be surprised that such a light-hearted, bustling restaurant lurks beyond the sleek lobby. Norma's menu is as playful as it is extensive, but the waitstaff knows their stuff, and they are always happy to guide you.

If you manage to garner one of the restaurant's coveted tables, you'll first be rewarded with a taste of the smoothie of the day. Then you will be served some of their outstanding coffee, which comes in an individual French press that a wait-person will constantly attend to throughout the meal—I was never able to beat him to the pour. From there, you can choose your feast. The menu at Norma's has its tongue firmly planted in its cheek, dividing dishes into categories such as "Eggs-Cellent" (the egg dishes), "The One That Didn't Get Away" (seafood-based dishes), and "Mom Can't Make This," glorious, artful presentations of traditional breakfast foods that no mother in her right mind would attempt. (See the "Wa-za?" in the "Royal Dishes" section, page 63.) I love my mother's French toast, but she's got nothing on the foie gras brioche French toast served at Norma's. It's beyond indulgent, and worth every calorie. Make sure someone at your table orders "The Wise Dr. Schmatikin's Mandarin Orange French Toast." The sweet/sour flavor of the mandarin oranges is a delightful counterpart to the fluffy battered bread.

All of Norma's dishes are fabulous, but some are unbelievable, like the "Zillion Dollar Lobster Frittata," served with either one ounce of sevruga caviar for $100 or ten ounces of the black gold for $1,000. Norma's even challenges your decadence with a note beneath the dish description that reads "Norma's dares you to expense this." It's this ebullient sense of humor that keeps Norma's from simply being a breakfast-themed restaurant. It is a jovial homage to the morning meal, taking breakfast and brunch dishes to new heights. With such huge portions of beautifully crafted food, you might start to consider breakfast as the new dinner.

Brunch Al Fresco

Three major brunch holidays (Easter, Mother's Day, and Father's Day) all fall on potentially warm, sunny days. But there's no need to wait for a special occasion to enjoy the great outdoors with your mimosa. Here are three of the best places to enjoy those eggs sunny side-out.

The street-side patio at **Aquagrill** (page 70) is surprisingly cozy. Somehow they've managed to block out the Sixth Avenue traffic with lovely flower boxes, and the impeccable service smooths over any remaining ruckus. But for the occasional taxi horn, you'd swear you were on a quiet, romantic street.

While I like the casual quality of breakfast at **Pastis** (page 53), it also serves a delicious brunch. The fashionista-watching from the sidewalk tables is unbeatable, and the food will transport you from the Meatpacking District to a Parisian café.

River Café (see page 108) doesn't exactly have outdoor seating. Instead, it has floor-to-ceiling windows that look across the river to the gorgeous Manhattan skyline. A clear view of the Statue of Liberty also makes for great scenery. On a sunny day, you feel like you're floating on the water in a yacht.

17. Ouest

Mouth-watering dishes at this new(ish) Upper Ouest Side favorite.

❋ BRUNCH HOURS:

Sunday 11 a.m.–2 p.m.

2315 Broadway (at 84th Street)

212-580-8700

Upper West Side

www.ouestny.com

Good for celebrations

Like its neighborhood buddy, Aix, Tom Valenti's Ouest dares to raise the standard of culinary excellence on the once gastronomically vapid Upper West Side. When most people think of brunch on the Upper West Side, they think of navigating a minefield of strollers to cram into a seat for passable pancakes. Ouest offers something a bit more refined. The second you walk into the lush, behemoth dining room, you'll know you're not at Sarabeth's anymore. Huge, round, Chianti-colored leather booths are swirled throughout the space, with backs high enough to keep your neighbors' conversations from intruding on your meal. The low ceiling fans whirring gently set a comfortable, unhurried pace for your dining experience. Even the kitchen action, which is on display in the open-kitchen design, is calmer than you'd expect. This confident, laissez-faire mood assures patrons that this is a restaurant that always gets it right.

When you sit down, you'll receive a bread basket of warm baked scones, muffins, and sweet rolls. Go for the buttery, flaky scones, which are especially good. The prix-fixe menu includes coffee or tea, but if you like a morning nip, try the Bellini. The peach puree is a sweet and fresh-tasting accompaniment to the bubbly Prosecco. The appetizers are delightfully unfussy (with choices like freshly made yogurt with dried cherries) and all of them are good, but it is the entrees that stand out at Ouest. (See the rolled omelette soufflé in the "Royal Dishes" section, page 64.) If you've never had a fried poached egg, give theirs a try. It is served with house-smoked duck breast. But all of the options are interesting, and made with fresh, top-quality ingredients, and the waitstaff, neatly dressed in gray vests with white shirts, make excellent recommendations in an almost conspiratorial tone. It's fun to be let in on their secrets. The large tables and chic atmosphere make Ouest a perfect place to celebrate any special occasion. Yes, it looks likes he's done it: Tom Valenti has conquered the Ouest Side.

18. Paris Commune

Vive la France, vive the French toast.

✳ BRUNCH HOURS:

Saturday and Sunday 10 a.m.–3:30 p.m.

99 Bank Street (at Greenwich Street)

212-929-0509

www.pariscommune.net

West Village

In November 2004, Paris Commune moved about half a block from its original location. Though it no longer has a wonderful fireplace, it has successfully managed to transport the rest of the cozy atmosphere to the new location. And if you ever stood in the long brunch lines at the old location, you'll be relieved to hear that there are more tables at the new one. With an attractive waitstaff and good, hearty French dishes, Paris Commune is a quintessential West Village haunt. The telltale sign that it belongs in the neighborhood is its popularity with hip neighbors like Marc Jacobs, who has a store around the corner.

The brunch menu is straightforward and there's something for everyone from health nuts to gluttons. I've seen several friends go into a kind ecstatic frenzy when they describe Paris Commune's French toast. But don't let that distract you from the silky omelettes or the crunchy granola. Now that Bleecker Street has become a shopping mecca, brunch at Paris Commune, which has been a fixture in the West Village for twenty-five years, is also a solid way to begin a day of shopping. You'll get your caffeine and protein, and, if Mr. Jacobs is sitting at the next table, maybe a dose of fashion inspiration.

19. Park Avenue Café

Refined American fare in an atmosphere that will please everyone, even your mother-in-law.

❖ BRUNCH HOURS:

Sunday 11 a.m.–2:30 p.m.

100 East 63rd Street (at Park Avenue)

212-644-1900

Upper East Side

www.parkavenuecafe.com

Good for celebrations

Park Avenue Café is to New York restaurants what Ralph Lauren is to fashion: dependable, beautifully tailored, but unafraid to give tradition a little jolt. One of the great things about Ralph Lauren is that his clothes are appropriate both for going out with your friends and for dinner with your grandparents. So it goes for Park Avenue Café. It is the perfect place to celebrate your Great Uncle Howie's eightieth birthday, or to have an intimate date with someone you want to impress.

Executive chef Neil Murphy's cooking career is said to have started aboard a U.S. naval submarine. From the way he commands a large kitchen to the consistency of what it turns out, you get a sense that he learned a thing or two in the galley. Brunch at Park Avenue Café is equal to its dinner, which is not always the case at some of New York's finest eateries. Start with the homemade jelly doughnuts with fruit salad. I think that people often dismiss the true wonder of a good homemade doughnut, because we've become inured by the less-than-wondrous corner deli versions. (See entry on the Doughnut Plant, page 32, for further discussion of the gourmet doughnut.) Park Avenue Café's jelly doughnuts are sublime. Also tasty in the appetizer department is the pastrami salmon and smoked salmon served with a warm corn blini. Moving on to the entrees, think about the rib-eye steak and egg served with potato and spinach charlotte. Park Avenue Café never skimps on its ingredients, and the steak here is flawless. If you dare, order it "black and blue" (charred on the outside, rare on the inside); this is a place you can feel perfectly safe doing so. If you didn't order the jelly doughnuts to start (or if you want a sugar rush), order the sweet raspberry, banana, and pecan waffles served with maple syrup and whipped yogurt. Crispy on the outside, moist on the inside, they're like ambrosia. And no matter what, make sure to order a side of salmon bacon for the table, because its salty goodness will be a great complement to any of the entrees.

Park Avenue Café has the space to hold private parties, and it's an excellent place to celebrate Father's Day. After brunch, walk over to the Central Park Zoo or to Madison Avenue for some window shopping. In fact, the restaurant is just a hop, skip, and a jump from Ralph Lauren.

20. Prune

An East Village gem with a funky flair.

✳ BRUNCH HOURS:

Saturday and Sunday 10 a.m.–3:30 p.m.

54 East 1st Street (between First and Second avenues)

212-677-6221

East Village

Prune is cool. I don't know how else to say it. It isn't pseudo-cool, it's actually cool. The space is cozy and unpretentious. The waitstaff are good-looking, but unlike the waifish model-like servers at other chic eateries who make you wonder when they last ate anything more substantial than a rice cake, you don't doubt they actually have eaten at Prune. The menu reflects its eclectic East Village location, and the Bloody Mary selection is extensive without being silly. It all works. So of course, everyone wants to be there. The waits for brunch can be brutal, but there is one sure way to deal with the some-times Kafkaesque line: Be cool. Remain cool. Relax. Hang out, grab a juice, and chat the minutes away. The wait is worth it.

Prune is chef Gabrielle Hamilton's childhood nickname; other than that, there's nothing about the restaurant that brings to mind the wrinkly fruit. Everything about Prune feels tight and fresh. Amazing cheeses and excellent smoked fish grace the menu courtesy of neighboring purveyors Joe's Dairy and Russ & Daughters. The Dutch-style pancake is dense and satisfying. It is at least an inch thick, and is topped with pears. Don't deny yourself the pleasures of the Monte Cristo, a ham and cheese sandwich that's battered and fried.

The waitstaff at Prune wear soft pink uniforms and seem to float around the tiny space. They are helpful and attentive without rushing you. However, seeing the line outside may make you feel less compelled to linger. Besides, after your delicious brunch, you'll probably want to do the cool thing and share the love.

21. Quintessence

Move over eggs Benedict, it's time for a raw brunch.

new york's 50 best places to enjoy breakfast and brunch

❊ BRUNCH HOURS:

Saturday and Sunday 11:30 a.m.–4 p.m.

353 East 78th Street (between First and Second avenues)

212-734-0888

Upper East Side

263 East 10th Street (between First and Avenue A)

646-654-1823

East Village

566 Amsterdam Avenue (at 87th Street)

212-501-9700

Upper West Side

www.quintessencerestaurant.com

Good for vegetarians and vegans

First, let me brief you on the principles of raw food: Raw food-ists believe that foods should be ingested in their natural form. By eating foods in their raw form, you don't jeopardize the benefits that come from the enzymes that are typically broken down when foods are heated to over 126 degrees. It's pretty much a vegan diet, uncooked (although Quintessence uses honey, which is not vegan but is raw). But don't worry, nobody at Quintessence is going to try to convince you to go raw. Instead, Quintessence can be an interesting introduction into the world of raw food, or simply a break from your nor-mal brunch routine.

Brunch is so often an excuse to eat heavy dishes; Quin-tessence sheds new light on what brunch can be. What's inter-esting about the food at Quintessence is that while it may draw inspiration from some cooked foods, it doesn't really attempt to recreate textures or flavors. The brunch menu is brief, but each choice is as interesting as the next. Start with a glass of nut milk made from soaked nuts, soy, honey, vanilla, and coconut water. It's smooth and interesting, and a nice choice for those who are lactose intolerant or for vegetarians looking for an alternative to soy milk. The fresh fruit crepe resembles a typical crepe, but the textures are coarser and the flavors are bolder. It's an excellent dish that's both energizing and pleasing. I was especially impressed by the nutty complexity of the granola. Quintessence is a raw food paradise that even a steak lover can enjoy.

22. River Café

A boathouse brunch with a million-dollar view.

new york's 50 best places to enjoy breakfast and brunch

❈ BRUNCH HOURS:

Sunday 11 a.m.–3 p.m.

1 Water Street

718-522-5200

Brooklyn Heights

www.rivercafe.com

Good for celebrations

When I set out to write this book, one of my self-imposed parameters was that I would limit myself to restaurants in Manhattan. I'm a Brooklynite, so I know that the city's gastronomic delights are not limited to Manhattan. Each borough could have its own guide, which is why, to limit it to fifty, I had to limit the territory. I have adhered to this limitation with the exception of River Café. Here's why: one of the restaurant's most impressive features is its view of Manhattan. Situated on the bank of the East River, River Café offers an unrivaled panorama of the Manhattan skyline. On a clear day, the view is mesmerizing. It conjures all of the warm, gushy "I love New York" feelings in you. So I don't think I'm really cheating here, because River Café is all about Manhattan. Fortunately, you don't have to ask for a window seat to enjoy the view; the restaurant has a wall of windows that you can gaze out of from almost every seat. If you are seated with your back to the window, encourage your dining companion to switch with you at some point; the view is worth the game of musical chairs.

The rest of the interior at this thirty-year-old restaurant is shabby-boathouse chic, reminiscent of a well-loved yacht club. The waitstaff wear suits and the service is old-fashioned in the wonderful, doting sense. All of this marks River Café's status as a New York City fixture.

Unlike some restaurants with a non-food-related signature feature, River Café has excellent food, and the elegant presentation of the dishes rivals the view. The prix-fixe menu features starters like hot-smoked rainbow trout served with fingerling potatoes, smoky bacon, white asparagus, and horseradish caviar sauce. Green papaya and chili lime dressing give the seared prime sirloin salad a refreshing Thai twist. Chef Brad Steelman's emphasis on contrasting textures is exemplified in the entree of slow-roasted suckling pig. The dish, served with maple sweet potatoes and a fried egg, is a study in contrasting consistencies, and the combination of the liquid yolk, the soft sweet potatoes, and the hearty pork make an already excellent dish stand out. River Café is also a good place to order eggs Benedict, because it doesn't mess with a good thing; perfectly cooked eggs are served with a warm, not-too-thick hollandaise. The one variation here is the use of brioche, which is an improvement on the traditional English muffin because it does a much better job of absorbing a broken yolk.

Don't skip the dessert. The chocolate marquise Brooklyn Bridge is actually constructed in the shape of the bridge you've been gazing at during your meal. It's a fun presentation and even more enjoyable to demolish with a spoon. After your meal, walk back to Manhattan over the Brooklyn Bridge. It's one of the best ways to enjoy the majesty of this great city.

23. Schiller's Liquor Bar

Pastis's and Balthazar's younger sibling lives up to its pedigree.

❄ BRUNCH HOURS:

Saturday and Sunday 10 a.m.–5 p.m.

131 Rivington Street (at Norfolk Street)

212-260-4555

Lower East Side

www.schillersny.com

Schiller's Liquor Bar is a perfect place to shake off the effects of a raucous Friday or Saturday night. Located in an old drugstore on the once-seedy-now-hip Lower East Side, Schiller's works hard to give you the impression that it has been around for a long time. The decor is a mishmash of French *fin de siècle* brasserie elements (see Balthazar and Pastis, pages 13 and 53 respectively), but the shiny white wall tile brightens up the dining room; during the day, and with the sun pouring in, it is practically cheery. If you've ever eaten dinner at Schiller's, you know that the nighttime crowd is mostly made up of rambunctious hipsters chowing down before a night out, but the brunch crowd is more subdued, and fortunately, so is the daytime atmosphere. After all, who wants to contend with more attitude and a frenzied atmosphere after an all-nighter.

The menu consists of a smattering of dishes from across the globe, hitting flavors from Mexico to England. There's Welsh rarebit, a rich and satisfying rendition of the classic British dish, with thick sliced bread topped with melted cheddar, a few crumbles of Stilton, and roasted tomatoes. The dense and chewy sour cream and hazelnut waffle is given a grown-up flair with mixed berries and a bourbon maple syrup. All of the egg dishes are first-rate. Eggs Hussard is a richer—yes, richer—version of classic eggs Benedict. Its combination of poached eggs with ham, mushrooms, *bordelaise* (a complex red wine sauce), and hollandaise will put you in a contented state. Schiller's steak frites also makes a superb brunch choice, as would the steak and eggs. There is something about consuming a steak before dinnertime that is daring and extravagant. And don't skip the pastries. Order the bread basket, with assorted breads and pastries from Balthazar Bakery, or try the freshly made "dollar doughnuts." They're the sweetest way to get a bang for your buck in the land of the up-and-coming.

After brunch, you can stroll around the neighborhood and see what new boutiques have cropped up, or make a reservation to go to the nearby Tenement Museum. Or do both and see what was, and what is to come.

24. Tartine

A sliver of the Left Bank nestled in the West Village.

❖ BRUNCH HOURS:
Saturday and Sunday 10:30 a.m.–4 p.m.
253 West 11th Street (at West Fourth Street)
212-229-2611
West Village

This cozy restaurant is located on a charming West Village street nestled among fabulous brownstones and town houses. Unlike her stately neighbors, Tartine is a little shabby—in a typically French laissez-faire kind of way—and about the size of an average New York studio apartment. No, maybe it's smaller. Still, it doesn't get more comfortable than Tartine, even when you're crammed elbow to elbow, and leaning forward every time the waiter squeezes past. You feel like you're dining in a room full of neighbors, which doesn't make you feel cramped—it makes you feel at home.

The brunch menu is short and sweet, and everything is yummy. Once you've tried the croque monsieur, you'll wonder if the restaurant's front door is really an entrance through a time-space continuum that leads straight to Paris. Made on homemade brioche, this is a faithful rendition of the traditional French sandwich, with a perfect balance of ham, cheese, and béchamel sauce. Forget Paris—that and a cup of the freshly brewed coffee may lead you straight to brunch nirvana. Many rave about the enormous apple pancake, which is light, fluffy, chock-full of apples, and large enough for a small army. The egg dishes are also good, and like many of the offerings are served with excellent roasted potatoes. Don't ignore the pastries: the pain au chocolat is heavenly, as are most of the baked treats.

There usually is a line to get in, but don't let the wait

deter you. I wouldn't recommend trying to bring a party of more than four—the dining room is miniscule—but with a newspaper, one companion, and the neighbors you'll meet in line, the wait will fly by.

Note: If you love the food, think about checking out **Miette Culinary Studio**, run by Tartine's chef, Paul Vandewoude. The classes, most of which are one session, focus on creating a single meal from three flavorful dishes. The evening classes are small (a maximum of twelve people), and they are held in a nineteenth-century West Village townhouse, so they are as intimate as a dining experience at Tartine. For more information, call 212-460-9322.

25. Town

Enjoy an elegant brunch with a touch of glamorous taste.

❄ BRUNCH HOURS:

Sunday 11 a.m.–3 p.m.

Chambers Hotel

15 West 56th Street (between Fifth and Sixth avenues)

212-582-4445

Midtown

www.townnyc.com

Good for celebrations

The dining room at Town is stunning and grand. When you walk down the stairs, you'll be surprised by how high the ceilings are—I'd guess at least two stories. It's roomy on the horizontal as well; unlike many popular brunch spots in New York, Town isn't packed with tables. But somehow, it doesn't feel cold, either. Instead, the lavish attention from the superb (and insanely handsome) staff makes each table feel like a private oasis.

Chef/owner Geoffrey Zakarian's menu echoes the chic warmth of the room. The dishes are simply composed, emphasizing the quality of the ingredients over complexity of preparation. The endive salad is, as the menu describes, "simply dressed" with olive oil and mustard. It's a refreshing change from the hyper-composed salads featured on so many menus these days. The endive, crisp and flavorful, is the star of this dish, and it gives an excellent performance. Moving on to the entrees, you'll find interesting variations on egg dishes, like the coddled eggs and short ribs. It is served with mush-rooms and mashed potatoes, which are melt-in-your-mouth delicious; the minimalist presentation of the dish is striking as well. The menu definitely hits some extravagant notes, such as the eggs served with a Kobe-beef flank steak, or the wonderful lobster hash with basted eggs and an olive oil hollandaise sauce.

In any other setting, the menu might feel a bit pretentious, but Town encourages you to be fashionable; just sitting there raises your level of sophistication a few notches. Still, for some, sitting in the ultra-cool room might make you feel like rebelling. In that case, by all means try the exceedingly good hamburger served with gingered coleslaw and butter chips.

✳ glossary
and
index

What's the difference between eggs Benedict and Florentine? What distinguishes Nova from lox? And what in the world is a crumpet anyway?

With breakfast and brunch menus come a whole lexicon beyond what you've learned on the back of your cereal box. Here's a quick rundown of some common terms, so you'll never have to puzzle over a morning-meal menu again.

bagel: a dense roll with a hole in the middle, traditionally boiled and then baked.

baked (or shirred) eggs: eggs broken into a baking dish and baked in an oven until set.

Belgian waffle: a thick, sweet waffle often served with ice cream, whipped cream, and/or fruit topping.

bialy: named for the Polish city, Bialystock, this roll is similar to a bagel, but rather than a hole it has a slight indentation in which sautéed chopped onions are sprinkled.

blintz: a thin pancake (similar to a crepe) traditionally filled with pot cheese and/or fruit.

Bloody Mary: a traditional brunch drink that is a mixture of tomato juice, vodka, and spices. It is thought to have originated at Harry's Bar in Paris.

brioche: a light but rich eggy bread.

Canadian bacon: trimmed, lean pressed pork loin, usually smoked.

clotted cream: thick cream made from scalded milk.

coddled eggs: eggs in the shell that are placed in boiling water to slightly cook or "coddle" them.

crème fraîche: a thick, slightly acidic (though not as sour as sour cream) cream.

croque monsieur: literally translated as "crunchy mister," this sandwich of French origin consists of a thick slice of soft cheese such as gruyere and a thin slice of ham between buttered bread that is toasted on both sides.

crumpet: similar to an English muffin, it is a type of thick, perforated pancake made from a yeasty batter.

dim sum: a selection of small Chinese dishes. In America, it often refers to a variety of dumplings.

eggs Benedict: poached eggs and Canadian bacon served on an English muffin with hollandaise sauce.

eggs Florentine: poached eggs and spinach served on an English muffin with hollandaise sauce.

eggs Norwegian: poached eggs and smoked salmon on an English muffin with hollandaise sauce.

flapjack: a griddle cake, traditionally made from oats, sugar, butter, and syrup.

French toast: slices of bread dipped or soaked in an egg batter and fried on both sides.

grits: coarsely ground hominy (corn kernels), cooked down in water and served with salt and butter.

herring: a fatty, fleshy fish from the Atlantic and Pacific; often pickled or creamed.

hollandaise sauce: a creamy sauce made from flour, butter, and eggs; the egg yolks give it a yellow hue.

huevos rancheros: a Mexican dish; typically fried eggs on tortillas with salsa, although there are many variations.

kippered: a term referring to a fish that has been split open, salted, and (usually) hot-smoked.

lox (or gravlax): A Scandinavian salt-cured salmon with a very delicate texture that is not smoked.

mimosa: a traditional brunch drink that is a mixture of champagne and orange juice.

Nova: originating in Nova Scotia, this is cold-smoked salmon of any type.

omelette: beaten eggs that are cooked until set without stirring; served with a variety of fillings.

over-easy eggs: fried eggs flipped over at the last moment so that the yolk is sealed in.

pain au chocolat: flaky pastry wrapped around chocolate.

pain perdu: literally "lost bread," it is the French name for French toast; the name refers to the idea that you revive "lost" or old bread with the egg batter that it is soaked in.

pancake: a flat cake made from a thin batter, fried on both sides on a griddle or in a skillet.

sable: smoked black cod.

schmear: from the Yiddish meaning "things that go together," it refers to a spread of cream cheese, usually on a bagel.

scone: a small biscuit made rich with eggs, butter, and cream; usually very dense and often flavored with fruits and/or nuts.

sturgeon: a flaky white fish that is usually smoked; also the source of one of the world's most coveted kinds of caviar.

sunny-side-up eggs: fried eggs, where the yolk is left loose.

waffle: pancakelike batter cooked in a specially designed iron, creating a thick, crunchy breakfast treat with a grid pattern on its surface.

breakfast and brunch index

new york's 50 best places to enjoy breakfast and brunch

breakfast and brunch neighborhood index

WEST VILLAGE

MEATPACKING DISTRICT

CHELSEA

FLATIRON, GRAMERCY, AND UNION SQUARE

MIDTOWN, HELL'S KITCHEN, AND GARMENT DISTRICT

UPPER EAST SIDE

UPPER WEST SIDE

HARLEM AND MORNINGSIDE HEIGHTS

BROOKLYN

About the Author

Courtney Baron is a playwright and morning meal connoisseur in New York City. She is the author of many articles and has been published in numerous anthologies. Always an avid lover of egg dishes, Courtney has always believed that the most important meal of the day should also be the most delicious.